2.9.95

ISBN 0-8373-1343-0

C-1343   CAREER EXAMINATION SERIES

W9-ARF-750

This is your
PASSBOOK® for...

Legal Secretary

Test Preparation Study Guide

Questions & Answers

NATIONAL LEARNING CORPORATION

PASSBOOK®
NOTICE

PASSBOOK® SERIES

THE *PASSBOOK® SERIES* has been created to prepare applicants and candidates for the ultimate academic battlefield — the examination room.

At some time in our lives, each and every one of us may be required to take an examination — for validation, matriculation, admission, qualification, registration, certification, or licensure.

Based on the assumption that every applicant or candidate has met the basic formal educational standards, has taken the required number of courses, and read the necessary texts, the *PASSBOOK® SERIES* furnishes the one special preparation which may assure passing with confidence, instead of failing with insecurity. Examination questions — together with answers — are furnished as the basic vehicle for study so that the mysteries of the examination and its compounding difficulties may be eliminated or diminished by a sure method.

This book is meant to help you pass your examination provided that you qualify and are serious in your objective.

The entire field is reviewed through the huge store of content information which is succinctly presented through a provocative and challenging approach — the question-and-answer method.

A climate of success is established by furnishing the correct answers at the end of each test.

You soon learn to recognize types of questions, forms of questions, and patterns of questioning. You may even begin to anticipate expected outcomes.

You perceive that many questions are repeated or adapted so that you can gain acute insights, which may enable you to score many sure points.

You learn how to confront new questions, or types of questions, and to attack them confidently and work out the correct answers.

You note objectives and emphases, and recognize pitfalls and dangers, so that you may make positive educational adjustments.

Moreover, you are kept fully informed in relation to new concepts, methods, practices, and directions in the field.

You discover that you are actually taking the examination all the time: you are preparing for the examination by "taking" an examination, not by reading extraneous and/or supererogatory textbooks.

In short, this PASSBOOK®, used directedly, should be an important factor in helping you to pass your test.

LEGAL SECRETARY

DUTIES

An employee in this class performs legal secretarial work. The incumbent must be familiar with legal terminology, legal format and procedures, and routine legal forms. The incumbent may also be responsible for routine secretarial and clerical duties such as filing, indexing, posting, proofreading and operating a small switchboard. The employee, if qualified, may be asked to take dictation, but stenographic skill is not a requirement for positions in the class. Work is performed in accordance with established procedures and employees work with some independence on routine assignments. All material is reviewed upon completion for content and accuracy, and related clerical work is periodically checked for accuracy. Does related work as required.

EXAMPLES OF TYPICAL TASKS

Takes and transcribes dictation of briefs, affidavits, affirmations, orders, certificates, notices, memoranda of law, letters and general memoranda. Relieves superior of administrative and office detail. Types legal documents, memoranda, reports, etc. Screens messages and telephone calls for superior. Indexes and files documents, letters and a variety of legal papers. Supervises employees of subordinate rank in the performance of secretarial and clerical tasks.

The written test will cover knowledge, skills, and/or abilities in such areas as:
1. Grammar/usage/punctuation;
2. Keyboarding practices;
3. Legal terminology, documents and forms;
4. Office practices; and
5. Spelling.

HOW TO TAKE A TEST

I. YOU MUST PASS AN EXAMINATION

A. WHAT EVERY CANDIDATE SHOULD KNOW

Examination applicants often ask us for help in preparing for the written test. What can I study in advance? What kinds of questions will be asked? How will the test be given? How will the papers be graded?

As an applicant for a civil service examination, you may be wondering about some of these things. Our purpose here is to suggest effective methods of advance study and to describe civil service examinations.

Your chances for success on this examination can be increased if you know how to prepare. Those "pre-examination jitters" can be reduced if you know what to expect. You can even experience an adventure in good citizenship if you know why civil service exams are given.

B. WHY ARE CIVIL SERVICE EXAMINATIONS GIVEN?

Civil service examinations are important to you in two ways. As a citizen, you want public jobs filled by employees who know how to do their work. As a job seeker, you want a fair chance to compete for that job on an equal footing with other candidates. The best-known means of accomplishing this two-fold goal is the competitive examination.

Exams are widely publicized throughout the nation. They may be administered for jobs in federal, state, city, municipal, town or village governments or agencies.

Any citizen may apply, with some limitations, such as the age or residence of applicants. Your experience and education may be reviewed to see whether you meet the requirements for the particular examination. When these requirements exist, they are reasonable and applied consistently to all applicants. Thus, a competitive examination may cause you some uneasiness now, but it is your privilege and safeguard.

C. HOW ARE CIVIL SERVICE EXAMS DEVELOPED?

Examinations are carefully written by trained technicians who are specialists in the field known as "psychological measurement," in consultation with recognized authorities in the field of work that the test will cover. These experts recommend the subject matter areas or skills to be tested; only those knowledges or skills important to your success on the job are included. The most reliable books and source materials available are used as references. Together, the experts and technicians judge the difficulty level of the questions.

Test technicians know how to phrase questions so that the problem is clearly stated. Their ethics do not permit "trick" or "catch" questions. Questions may have been tried out on sample groups, or subjected to statistical analysis, to determine their usefulness.

Written tests are often used in combination with performance tests, ratings of training and experience, and oral interviews. All of these measures combine to form the best-known means of finding the right person for the right job.

II. HOW TO PASS THE WRITTEN TEST

A. NATURE OF THE EXAMINATION

To prepare intelligently for civil service examinations, you should know how they differ from school examinations you have taken. In school you were assigned certain definite pages to read or subjects to cover. The examination questions were quite detailed and usually emphasized memory. Civil service exams, on the other hand, try to discover your present ability to perform the duties of a position, plus your potentiality to learn these duties. In other words, a civil service exam attempts to predict how successful you will be. Questions cover such a broad area that they cannot be as minute and detailed as school exam questions.

In the public service similar kinds of work, or positions, are grouped together in one "class." This process is known as *position-classification*. All the positions in a class are paid according to the salary range for that class. One class title covers all of these positions, and they are all tested by the same examination.

B. FOUR BASIC STEPS

1) Study the announcement

How, then, can you know what subjects to study? Our best answer is: "Learn as much as possible about the class of positions for which you've applied." The exam will test the knowledge, skills and abilities needed to do the work.

Your most valuable source of information about the position you want is the official exam announcement. This announcement lists the training and experience qualifications. Check these standards and apply only if you come reasonably close to meeting them.

The brief description of the position in the examination announcement offers some clues to the subjects which will be tested. Think about the job itself. Review the duties in your mind. Can you perform them, or are there some in which you are rusty? Fill in the blank spots in your preparation.

Many jurisdictions preview the written test in the exam announcement by including a section called "Knowledge and Abilities Required," "Scope of the Examination," or some similar heading. Here you will find out specifically what fields will be tested.

2) Review your own background

Once you learn in general what the position is all about, and what you need to know to do the work, ask yourself which subjects you already know fairly well and which need improvement. You may wonder whether to concentrate on improving your strong areas or on building some background in your fields of weakness. When the announcement has specified "some knowledge" or "considerable knowledge," or has used adjectives like "beginning principles of..." or "advanced ... methods," you can get a clue as to the number and difficulty of questions to be asked in any given field. More questions, and hence broader coverage, would be included for those subjects which are more important in the work. Now weigh your strengths and weaknesses against the job requirements and prepare accordingly.

3) Determine the level of the position

Another way to tell how intensively you should prepare is to understand the level of the job for which you are applying. Is it the entering level? In other words, is this the position in which beginners in a field of work are hired? Or is it an intermediate or

2

advanced level? Sometimes this is indicated by such words as "Junior" or "Senior" in the class title. Other jurisdictions use Roman numerals to designate the level – Clerk I, Clerk II, for example. The word "Supervisor" sometimes appears in the title. If the level is not indicated by the title, check the description of duties. Will you be working under very close supervision, or will you have responsibility for independent decisions in this work?

4) Choose appropriate study materials

Now that you know the subjects to be examined and the relative amount of each subject to be covered, you can choose suitable study materials. For beginning level jobs, or even advanced ones, if you have a pronounced weakness in some aspect of your training, read a modern, standard textbook in that field. Be sure it is up to date and has general coverage. Such books are normally available at your library, and the librarian will be glad to help you locate one. For entry-level positions, questions of appropriate difficulty are chosen – neither highly advanced questions, nor those too simple. Such questions require careful thought but not advanced training.

If the position for which you are applying is technical or advanced, you will read more advanced, specialized material. If you are already familiar with the basic principles of your field, elementary textbooks would waste your time. Concentrate on advanced textbooks and technical periodicals. Think through the concepts and review difficult problems in your field.

These are all general sources. You can get more ideas on your own initiative, following these leads. For example, training manuals and publications of the government agency which employs workers in your field can be useful, particularly for technical and professional positions. A letter or visit to the government department involved may result in more specific study suggestions, and certainly will provide you with a more definite idea of the exact nature of the position you are seeking.

III. KINDS OF TESTS

Tests are used for purposes other than measuring knowledge and ability to perform specified duties. For some positions, it is equally important to test ability to make adjustments to new situations or to profit from training. In others, basic mental abilities not dependent on information are essential. Questions which test these things may not appear as pertinent to the duties of the position as those which test for knowledge and information. Yet they are often highly important parts of a fair examination. For very general questions, it is almost impossible to help you direct your study efforts. What we can do is to point out some of the more common of these general abilities needed in public service positions and describe some typical questions.

1) General information

Broad, general information has been found useful for predicting job success in some kinds of work. This is tested in a variety of ways, from vocabulary lists to questions about current events. Basic background in some field of work, such as sociology or economics, may be sampled in a group of questions. Often these are principles which have become familiar to most persons through exposure rather than through formal training. It is difficult to advise you how to study for these questions; being alert to the world around you is our best suggestion.

2) Verbal ability

An example of an ability needed in many positions is verbal or language ability. Verbal ability is, in brief, the ability to use and understand words. Vocabulary and grammar tests are typical measures of this ability. Reading comprehension or paragraph interpretation questions are common in many kinds of civil service tests. You are given a paragraph of written material and asked to find its central meaning.

3) Numerical ability

Number skills can be tested by the familiar arithmetic problem, by checking paired lists of numbers to see which are alike and which are different, or by interpreting charts and graphs. In the latter test, a graph may be printed in the test booklet which you are asked to use as the basis for answering questions.

4) Observation

A popular test for law-enforcement positions is the observation test. A picture is shown to you for several minutes, then taken away. Questions about the picture test your ability to observe both details and larger elements.

5) Following directions

In many positions in the public service, the employee must be able to carry out written instructions dependably and accurately. You may be given a chart with several columns, each column listing a variety of information. The questions require you to carry out directions involving the information given in the chart.

6) Skills and aptitudes

Performance tests effectively measure some manual skills and aptitudes. When the skill is one in which you are trained, such as typing or shorthand, you can practice. These tests are often very much like those given in business school or high school courses. For many of the other skills and aptitudes, however, no short-time preparation can be made. Skills and abilities natural to you or that you have developed throughout your lifetime are being tested.

Many of the general questions just described provide all the data needed to answer the questions and ask you to use your reasoning ability to find the answers. Your best preparation for these tests, as well as for tests of facts and ideas, is to be at your physical and mental best. You, no doubt, have your own methods of getting into an exam-taking mood and keeping "in shape." The next section lists some ideas on this subject.

IV. KINDS OF QUESTIONS

Only rarely is the "essay" question, which you answer in narrative form, used in civil service tests. Civil service tests are usually of the short-answer type. Full instructions for answering these questions will be given to you at the examination. But in case this is your first experience with short-answer questions and separate answer sheets, here is what you need to know:

1) Multiple-choice Questions

Most popular of the short-answer questions is the "multiple choice" or "best answer" question. It can be used, for example, to test for factual knowledge, ability to solve problems or judgment in meeting situations found at work.

A multiple-choice question is normally one of three types—

- It can begin with an incomplete statement followed by several possible endings. You are to find the one ending which *best* completes the statement, although some of the others may not be entirely wrong.
- It can also be a complete statement in the form of a question which is answered by choosing one of the statements listed.
- It can be in the form of a problem – again you select the best answer.

Here is an example of a multiple-choice question with a discussion which should give you some clues as to the method for choosing the right answer:

When an employee has a complaint about his assignment, the action which will *best* help him overcome his difficulty is to
- A. discuss his difficulty with his coworkers
- B. take the problem to the head of the organization
- C. take the problem to the person who gave him the assignment
- D. say nothing to anyone about his complaint

In answering this question, you should study each of the choices to find which is best. Consider choice "A" – Certainly an employee may discuss his complaint with fellow employees, but no change or improvement can result, and the complaint remains unresolved. Choice "B" is a poor choice since the head of the organization probably does not know what assignment you have been given, and taking your problem to him is known as "going over the head" of the supervisor. The supervisor, or person who made the assignment, is the person who can clarify it or correct any injustice. Choice "C" is, therefore, correct. To say nothing, as in choice "D," is unwise. Supervisors have and interest in knowing the problems employees are facing, and the employee is seeking a solution to his problem.

2) True/False Questions

The "true/false" or "right/wrong" form of question is sometimes used. Here a complete statement is given. Your job is to decide whether the statement is right or wrong.

SAMPLE: A person-to-person long-distance telephone call costs less than a station-to-station call to the same city.

This statement is wrong, or false, since person-to-person calls are more expensive.

This is not a complete list of all possible question forms, although most of the others are variations of these common types. You will always get complete directions for answering questions. Be sure you understand *how* to mark your answers – ask questions until you do.

V. RECORDING YOUR ANSWERS

For an examination with very few applicants, you may be told to record your answers in the test booklet itself. Separate answer sheets are much more common. If this separate answer sheet is to be scored by machine – and this is often the case – it is highly important that you mark your answers correctly in order to get credit.

An electric scoring machine is often used in civil service offices because of the speed with which papers can be scored. Machine-scored answer sheets must be marked with a pencil, which will be given to you. This pencil has a high graphite content which responds to the electric scoring machine. As a matter of fact, stray dots may register as answers, so do not let your pencil rest on the answer sheet while you are pondering the correct answer. Also, if your pencil lead breaks or is otherwise defective, ask for another.

Since the answer sheet will be dropped in a slot in the scoring machine, be careful not to bend the corners or get the paper crumpled.

The answer sheet normally has five vertical columns of numbers, with 30 numbers to a column. These numbers correspond to the question numbers in your test booklet. After each number, going across the page are four or five pairs of dotted lines. These short dotted lines have small letters or numbers above them. The first two pairs may also have a "T" or "F" above the letters. This indicates that the first two pairs only are to be used if the questions are of the true-false type. If the questions are multiple choice, disregard the "T" and "F" and pay attention only to the small letters or numbers.

Answer your questions in the manner of the sample that follows:

32. The largest city in the United States is
    A. Washington, D.C.
    B. New York City
    C. Chicago
    D. Detroit
    E. San Francisco

1) Choose the answer you think is best. (New York City is the largest, so "B" is correct.)
2) Find the row of dotted lines numbered the same as the question you are answering. (Find row number 32)
3) Find the pair of dotted lines corresponding to the answer. (Find the pair of lines under the mark "B.")
4) Make a solid black mark between the dotted lines.

VI. BEFORE THE TEST

Common sense will help you find procedures to follow to get ready for an examination. Too many of us, however, overlook these sensible measures. Indeed, nervousness and fatigue have been found to be the most serious reasons why applicants fail to do their best on civil service tests. Here is a list of reminders:

- Begin your preparation early – Don't wait until the last minute to go scurrying around for books and materials or to find out what the position is all about.
- Prepare continuously – An hour a night for a week is better than an all-night cram session. This has been definitely established. What is more, a night a

week for a month will return better dividends than crowding your study into a shorter period of time.

- Locate the place of the exam – You have been sent a notice telling you when and where to report for the examination. If the location is in a different town or otherwise unfamiliar to you, it would be well to inquire the best route and learn something about the building.
- Relax the night before the test – Allow your mind to rest. Do not study at all that night. Plan some mild recreation or diversion; then go to bed early and get a good night's sleep.
- Get up early enough to make a leisurely trip to the place for the test – This way unforeseen events, traffic snarls, unfamiliar buildings, etc. will not upset you.
- Dress comfortably – A written test is not a fashion show. You will be known by number and not by name, so wear something comfortable.
- Leave excess paraphernalia at home – Shopping bags and odd bundles will get in your way. You need bring only the items mentioned in the official notice you received; usually everything you need is provided. Do not bring reference books to the exam. They will only confuse those last minutes and be taken away from you when in the test room.
- Arrive somewhat ahead of time – If because of transportation schedules you must get there very early, bring a newspaper or magazine to take your mind off yourself while waiting.
- Locate the examination room – When you have found the proper room, you will be directed to the seat or part of the room where you will sit. Sometimes you are given a sheet of instructions to read while you are waiting. Do not fill out any forms until you are told to do so; just read them and be prepared.
- Relax and prepare to listen to the instructions
- If you have any physical problem that may keep you from doing your best, be sure to tell the test administrator. If you are sick or in poor health, you really cannot do your best on the exam. You can come back and take the test some other time.

VII. AT THE TEST

The day of the test is here and you have the test booklet in your hand. The temptation to get going is very strong. Caution! There is more to success than knowing the right answers. You must know how to identify your papers and understand variations in the type of short-answer question used in this particular examination. Follow these suggestions for maximum results from your efforts:

1) Cooperate with the monitor
The test administrator has a duty to create a situation in which you can be as much at ease as possible. He will give instructions, tell you when to begin, check to see that you are marking your answer sheet correctly, and so on. He is not there to guard you, although he will see that your competitors do not take unfair advantage. He wants to help you do your best.

2) Listen to all instructions
Don't jump the gun! Wait until you understand all directions. In most civil service tests you get more time than you need to answer the questions. So don't be in a hurry.

Read each word of instructions until you clearly understand the meaning. Study the examples, listen to all announcements and follow directions. Ask questions if you do not understand what to do.

3) Identify your papers

Civil service exams are usually identified by number only. You will be assigned a number; you must not put your name on your test papers. Be sure to copy your number correctly. Since more than one exam may be given, copy your exact examination title.

4) Plan your time

Unless you are told that a test is a "speed" or "rate of work" test, speed itself is usually not important. Time enough to answer all the questions will be provided, but this does not mean that you have all day. An overall time limit has been set. Divide the total time (in minutes) by the number of questions to determine the approximate time you have for each question.

5) Do not linger over difficult questions

If you come across a difficult question, mark it with a paper clip (useful to have along) and come back to it when you have been through the booklet. One caution if you do this – be sure to skip a number on your answer sheet as well. Check often to be sure that you have not lost your place and that you are marking in the row numbered the same as the question you are answering.

6) Read the questions

Be sure you know what the question asks! Many capable people are unsuccessful because they failed to *read* the questions correctly.

7) Answer all questions

Unless you have been instructed that a penalty will be deducted for incorrect answers, it is better to guess than to omit a question.

8) Speed tests

It is often better NOT to guess on speed tests. It has been found that on timed tests people are tempted to spend the last few seconds before time is called in marking answers at random – without even reading them – in the hope of picking up a few extra points. To discourage this practice, the instructions may warn you that your score will be "corrected" for guessing. That is, a penalty will be applied. The incorrect answers will be deducted from the correct ones, or some other penalty formula will be used.

9) Review your answers

If you finish before time is called, go back to the questions you guessed or omitted to give them further thought. Review other answers if you have time.

10) Return your test materials

If you are ready to leave before others have finished or time is called, take ALL your materials to the monitor and leave quietly. Never take any test material with you. The monitor can discover whose papers are not complete, and taking a test booklet may be grounds for disqualification.

VIII. EXAMINATION TECHNIQUES

1) Read the general instructions carefully. These are usually printed on the first page of the exam booklet. As a rule, these instructions refer to the timing of the examination; the fact that you should not start work until the signal and must stop work at a signal, etc. If there are any *special* instructions, such as a choice of questions to be answered, make sure that you note this instruction carefully.

2) When you are ready to start work on the examination, that is as soon as the signal has been given, read the instructions to each question booklet, underline any key words or phrases, such as *least, best, outline, describe* and the like. In this way you will tend to answer as requested rather than discover on reviewing your paper that you *listed without describing*, that you selected the *worst* choice rather than the *best* choice, etc.

3) If the examination is of the objective or multiple-choice type – that is, each question will also give a series of possible answers: A, B, C or D, and you are called upon to select the best answer and write the letter next to that answer on your answer paper – it is advisable to start answering each question in turn. There may be anywhere from 50 to 100 such questions in the three or four hours allotted and you can see how much time would be taken if you read through all the questions before beginning to answer any. Furthermore, if you come across a question or group of questions which you know would be difficult to answer, it would undoubtedly affect your handling of all the other questions.

4) If the examination is of the essay type and contains but a few questions, it is a moot point as to whether you should read all the questions before starting to answer any one. Of course, if you are given a choice – say five out of seven and the like – then it is essential to read all the questions so you can eliminate the two that are most difficult. If, however, you are asked to answer all the questions, there may be danger in trying to answer the easiest one first because you may find that you will spend too much time on it. The best technique is to answer the first question, then proceed to the second, etc.

5) Time your answers. Before the exam begins, write down the time it started, then add the time allowed for the examination and write down the time it must be completed, then divide the time available somewhat as follows:
   - If 3-1/2 hours are allowed, that would be 210 minutes. If you have 80 objective-type questions, that would be an average of 2-1/2 minutes per question. Allow yourself no more than 2 minutes per question, or a total of 160 minutes, which will permit about 50 minutes to review.
   - If for the time allotment of 210 minutes there are 7 essay questions to answer, that would average about 30 minutes a question. Give yourself only 25 minutes per question so that you have about 35 minutes to review.

6) The most important instruction is to *read each question* and make sure you know what is wanted. The second most important instruction is to *time yourself properly* so that you answer every question. The third most

9

important instruction is to *answer every question*. Guess if you have to but include something for each question. Remember that you will receive no credit for a blank and will probably receive some credit if you write something in answer to an essay question. If you guess a letter – say "B" for a multiple-choice question – you may have guessed right. If you leave a blank as an answer to a multiple-choice question, the examiners may respect your feelings but it will not add a point to your score. Some exams may penalize you for wrong answers, so in such cases *only*, you may not want to guess unless you have some basis for your answer.

7) Suggestions
   a. Objective-type questions
      1. Examine the question booklet for proper sequence of pages and questions
      2. Read all instructions carefully
      3. Skip any question which seems too difficult; return to it after all other questions have been answered
      4. Apportion your time properly; do not spend too much time on any single question or group of questions
      5. Note and underline key words – *all, most, fewest, least, best, worst, same, opposite,* etc.
      6. Pay particular attention to negatives
      7. Note unusual option, e.g., unduly long, short, complex, different or similar in content to the body of the question
      8. Observe the use of "hedging" words – *probably, may, most likely,* etc.
      9. Make sure that your answer is put next to the same number as the question .
      10. Do not second-guess unless you have good reason to believe the second answer is definitely more correct
      11. Cross out original answer if you decide another answer is more accurate; do not erase until you are ready to hand your paper in
      12. Answer all questions; guess unless instructed otherwise
      13. Leave time for review

   b. Essay questions
      1. Read each question carefully
      2. Determine exactly what is wanted. Underline key words or phrases.
      3. Decide on outline or paragraph answer
      4. Include many different points and elements unless asked to develop any one or two points or elements
      5. Show impartiality by giving pros and cons unless directed to select one side only
      6. Make and write down any assumptions you find necessary to answer the questions
      7. Watch your English, grammar, punctuation and choice of words
      8. Time your answers; don't crowd material

8) Answering the essay question

Most essay questions can be answered by framing the specific response around several key words or ideas. Here are a few such key words or ideas:

M's: manpower, materials, methods, money, management
P's: purpose, program, policy, plan, procedure, practice, problems, pitfalls, personnel, public relations

    a. Six basic steps in handling problems:
1. Preliminary plan and background development
2. Collect information, data and facts
3. Analyze and interpret information, data and facts
4. Analyze and develop solutions as well as make recommendations
5. Prepare report and sell recommendations
6. Install recommendations and follow up effectiveness

    b. Pitfalls to avoid
1. *Taking things for granted* – A statement of the situation does not necessarily imply that each of the elements is necessarily true; for example, a complaint may be invalid and biased so that all that can be taken for granted is that a complaint has been registered
2. *Considering only one side of a situation* – Wherever possible, indicate several alternatives and then point out the reasons you selected the best one
3. *Failing to indicate follow up* – Whenever your answer indicates action on your part, make certain that you will take proper follow-up action to see how successful your recommendations, procedures or actions turn out to be
4. *Taking too long in answering any single question* – Remember to time your answers properly

IX. AFTER THE TEST

Scoring procedures differ in detail among civil service jurisdictions although the general principles are the same. Whether the papers are hand-scored or graded by machine we have described, they are nearly always graded by number. That is, the person who marks the paper knows only the number – never the name – of the applicant. Not until all the papers have been graded will they be matched with names. If other tests, such as training and experience or oral interview ratings have been given, scores will be combined. Different parts of the examination usually have different weights. For example, the written test might count 60 percent of the final grade, and a rating of training and experience 40 percent. In many jurisdictions, veterans will have a certain number of points added to their grades.

After the final grade has been determined, the names are placed in grade order and an eligible list is established. There are various methods for resolving ties between those who get the same final grade – probably the most common is to place first the name of the person whose application was received first. Job offers are made from the eligible list in the order the names appear on it. You will be notified of your grade and your rank as soon as all these computations have been made. This will be done as rapidly as possible.

People who are found to meet the requirements in the announcement are called "eligibles." Their names are put on a list of eligible candidates. An eligible's chances of getting a job depend on how high he stands on this list and how fast agencies are filling jobs from the list.

When a job is to be filled from a list of eligibles, the agency asks for the names of people on the list of eligibles for that job. When the civil service commission receives this request, it sends to the agency the names of the three people highest on this list. Or, if the job to be filled has specialized requirements, the office sends the agency the names of the top three persons who meet these requirements from the general list.

The appointing officer makes a choice from among the three people whose names were sent to him. If the selected person accepts the appointment, the names of the others are put back on the list to be considered for future openings.

That is the rule in hiring from all kinds of eligible lists, whether they are for typist, carpenter, chemist, or something else. For every vacancy, the appointing officer has his choice of any one of the top three eligibles on the list. This explains why the person whose name is on top of the list sometimes does not get an appointment when some of the persons lower on the list do. If the appointing officer chooses the second or third eligible, the No. 1 eligible does not get a job at once, but stays on the list until he is appointed or the list is terminated.

X. HOW TO PASS THE INTERVIEW TEST

The examination for which you applied requires an oral interview test. You have already taken the written test and you are now being called for the interview test – the final part of the formal examination.

You may think that it is not possible to prepare for an interview test and that there are no procedures to follow during an interview. Our purpose is to point out some things you can do in advance that will help you and some good rules to follow and pitfalls to avoid while you are being interviewed.

What is an interview supposed to test?

The written examination is designed to test the technical knowledge and competence of the candidate; the oral is designed to evaluate intangible qualities, not readily measured otherwise, and to establish a list showing the relative fitness of each candidate – as measured against his competitors – for the position sought. Scoring is not on the basis of "right" and "wrong," but on a sliding scale of values ranging from "not passable" to "outstanding." As a matter of fact, it is possible to achieve a relatively low score without a single "incorrect" answer because of evident weakness in the qualities being measured.

Occasionally, an examination may consist entirely of an oral test – either an individual or a group oral. In such cases, information is sought concerning the technical knowledges and abilities of the candidate, since there has been no written examination for this purpose. More commonly, however, an oral test is used to supplement a written examination.

Who conducts interviews?

The composition of oral boards varies among different jurisdictions. In nearly all, a representative of the personnel department serves as chairman. One of the members of the board may be a representative of the department in which the candidate would work. In some cases, "outside experts" are used, and, frequently, a businessman or some other representative of the general public is asked to serve. Labor and management or other special groups may be represented. The aim is to secure the services of experts in the appropriate field.

However the board is composed, it is a good idea (and not at all improper or unethical) to ascertain in advance of the interview who the members are and what groups they represent. When you are introduced to them, you will have some idea of their backgrounds and interests, and at least you will not stutter and stammer over their names.

What should be done before the interview?

While knowledge about the board members is useful and takes some of the surprise element out of the interview, there is other preparation which is more substantive. It *is* possible to prepare for an oral interview – in several ways:

1) Keep a copy of your application and review it carefully before the interview

This may be the only document before the oral board, and the starting point of the interview. Know what education and experience you have listed there, and the sequence and dates of all of it. Sometimes the board will ask you to review the highlights of your experience for them; you should not have to hem and haw doing it.

2) Study the class specification and the examination announcement

Usually, the oral board has one or both of these to guide them. The qualities, characteristics or knowledges required by the position sought are stated in these documents. They offer valuable clues as to the nature of the oral interview. For example, if the job involves supervisory responsibilities, the announcement will usually indicate that knowledge of modern supervisory methods and the qualifications of the candidate as a supervisor will be tested. If so, you can expect such questions, frequently in the form of a hypothetical situation which you are expected to solve. NEVER go into an oral without knowledge of the duties and responsibilities of the job you seek.

3) Think through each qualification required

Try to visualize the kind of questions you would ask if you were a board member. How well could you answer them? Try especially to appraise your own knowledge and background in each area, *measured against the job sought*, and identify any areas in which you are weak. Be critical and realistic – do not flatter yourself.

4) Do some general reading in areas in which you feel you may be weak

For example, if the job involves supervision and your past experience has NOT, some general reading in supervisory methods and practices, particularly in the field of human relations, might be useful. Do NOT study agency procedures or detailed manuals. The oral board will be testing your understanding and capacity, not your memory.

5) Get a good night's sleep and watch your general health and mental attitude

You will want a clear head at the interview. Take care of a cold or any other minor ailment, and of course, no hangovers.

What should be done on the day of the interview?

Now comes the day of the interview itself. Give yourself plenty of time to get there. Plan to arrive somewhat ahead of the scheduled time, particularly if your appointment is in the fore part of the day. If a previous candidate fails to appear, the board might be ready for you a bit early. By early afternoon an oral board is almost invariably behind schedule if there are many candidates, and you may have to wait.

Take along a book or magazine to read, or your application to review, but leave any extraneous material in the waiting room when you go in for your interview. In any event, relax and compose yourself.

The matter of dress is important. The board is forming impressions about you – from your experience, your manners, your attitude, and your appearance. Give your personal appearance careful attention. Dress your best, but not your flashiest. Choose conservative, appropriate clothing, and be sure it is immaculate. This is a business interview, and your appearance should indicate that you regard it as such. Besides, being well groomed and properly dressed will help boost your confidence.

Sooner or later, someone will call your name and escort you into the interview room. *This is it.* From here on you are on your own. It is too late for any more preparation. But remember, you asked for this opportunity to prove your fitness, and you are here because your request was granted.

What happens when you go in?
The usual sequence of events will be as follows: The clerk (who is often the board stenographer) will introduce you to the chairman of the oral board, who will introduce you to the other members of the board. Acknowledge the introductions before you sit down. Do not be surprised if you find a microphone facing you or a stenotypist sitting by. Oral interviews are usually recorded in the event of an appeal or other review.

Usually the chairman of the board will open the interview by reviewing the highlights of your education and work experience from your application – primarily for the benefit of the other members of the board, as well as to get the material into the record. Do not interrupt or comment unless there is an error or significant misinterpretation; if that is the case, do not hesitate. But do not quibble about insignificant matters. Also, he will usually ask you some question about your education, experience or your present job – partly to get you to start talking and to establish the interviewing "rapport." He may start the actual questioning, or turn it over to one of the other members. Frequently, each member undertakes the questioning on a particular area, one in which he is perhaps most competent, so you can expect each member to participate in the examination. Because time is limited, you may also expect some rather abrupt switches in the direction the questioning takes, so do not be upset by it. Normally, a board member will not pursue a single line of questioning unless he discovers a particular strength or weakness.

After each member has participated, the chairman will usually ask whether any member has any further questions, then will ask you if you have anything you wish to add. Unless you are expecting this question, it may floor you. Worse, it may start you off on an extended, extemporaneous speech. The board is not usually seeking more information. The question is principally to offer you a last opportunity to present further qualifications or to indicate that you have nothing to add. So, if you feel that a significant qualification or characteristic has been overlooked, it is proper to point it out in a sentence or so. Do not compliment the board on the thoroughness of their examination – they have been sketchy, and you know it. If you wish, merely say, "No thank you, I have nothing further to add." This is a point where you can "talk yourself out" of a good impression or fail to present an important bit of information. Remember, *you close the interview yourself.*

The chairman will then say, "That is all, Mr. _____, thank you." Do not be startled; the interview is over, and quicker than you think. Thank him, gather your belongings and take your leave. Save your sigh of relief for the other side of the door.

How to put your best foot forward

Throughout this entire process, you may feel that the board individually and collectively is trying to pierce your defenses, seek out your hidden weaknesses and embarrass and confuse you. Actually, this is not true. They are obliged to make an appraisal of your qualifications for the job you are seeking, and they want to see you in your best light. Remember, they must interview all candidates and a non-cooperative candidate may become a failure in spite of their best efforts to bring out his qualifications. Here are 15 suggestions that will help you:

1) Be natural – Keep your attitude confident, not cocky

If you are not confident that you can do the job, do not expect the board to be. Do not apologize for your weaknesses, try to bring out your strong points. The board is interested in a positive, not negative, presentation. Cockiness will antagonize any board member and make him wonder if you are covering up a weakness by a false show of strength.

2) Get comfortable, but don't lounge or sprawl

Sit erectly but not stiffly. A careless posture may lead the board to conclude that you are careless in other things, or at least that you are not impressed by the importance of the occasion. Either conclusion is natural, even if incorrect. Do not fuss with your clothing, a pencil or an ashtray. Your hands may occasionally be useful to emphasize a point; do not let them become a point of distraction.

3) Do not wisecrack or make small talk

This is a serious situation, and your attitude should show that you consider it as such. Further, the time of the board is limited – they do not want to waste it, and neither should you.

4) Do not exaggerate your experience or abilities

In the first place, from information in the application or other interviews and sources, the board may know more about you than you think. Secondly, you probably will not get away with it. An experienced board is rather adept at spotting such a situation, so do not take the chance.

5) If you know a board member, do not make a point of it, yet do not hide it

Certainly you are not fooling him, and probably not the other members of the board. Do not try to take advantage of your acquaintanceship – it will probably do you little good.

6) Do not dominate the interview

Let the board do that. They will give you the clues – do not assume that you have to do all the talking. Realize that the board has a number of questions to ask you, and do not try to take up all the interview time by showing off your extensive knowledge of the answer to the first one.

7) Be attentive

You only have 20 minutes or so, and you should keep your attention at its sharpest throughout. When a member is addressing a problem or question to you, give him your undivided attention. Address your reply principally to him, but do not exclude the other board members.

8) Do not interrupt

A board member may be stating a problem for you to analyze. He will ask you a question when the time comes. Let him state the problem, and wait for the question.

9) Make sure you understand the question

Do not try to answer until you are sure what the question is. If it is not clear, restate it in your own words or ask the board member to clarify it for you. However, do not haggle about minor elements.

10) Reply promptly but not hastily

A common entry on oral board rating sheets is "candidate responded readily," or "candidate hesitated in replies." Respond as promptly and quickly as you can, but do not jump to a hasty, ill-considered answer.

11) Do not be peremptory in your answers

A brief answer is proper – but do not fire your answer back. That is a losing game from your point of view. The board member can probably ask questions much faster than you can answer them.

12) Do not try to create the answer you think the board member wants

He is interested in what kind of mind you have and how it works – not in playing games. Furthermore, he can usually spot this practice and will actually grade you down on it.

13) Do not switch sides in your reply merely to agree with a board member

Frequently, a member will take a contrary position merely to draw you out and to see if you are willing and able to defend your point of view. Do not start a debate, yet do not surrender a good position. If a position is worth taking, it is worth defending.

14) Do not be afraid to admit an error in judgment if you are shown to be wrong

The board knows that you are forced to reply without any opportunity for careful consideration. Your answer may be demonstrably wrong. If so, admit it and get on with the interview.

15) Do not dwell at length on your present job

The opening question may relate to your present assignment. Answer the question but do not go into an extended discussion. You are being examined for a *new* job, not your present one. As a matter of fact, try to phrase ALL your answers in terms of the job for which you are being examined.

Basis of Rating

Probably you will forget most of these "do's" and "don'ts" when you walk into the oral interview room. Even remembering them all will not ensure you a passing grade. Perhaps you did not have the qualifications in the first place. But remembering them will help you to put your best foot forward, without treading on the toes of the board members.

Rumor and popular opinion to the contrary notwithstanding, an oral board wants you to make the best appearance possible. They know you are under pressure – but they also want to see how you respond to it as a guide to what your reaction would be under the pressures of the job you seek. They will be influenced by the degree of poise you display, the personal traits you show and the manner in which you respond.

EXAMINATION SECTION

EXAMINATION SECTION
TEST 1

DIRECTIONS: Each question or incomplete statement is followed by several suggested answers or completions. Select the one that BEST answers the question or completes the statement. *PRINT THE LETTER OF THE CORRECT ANSWER IN THE SPACE AT THE RIGHT.*

Questions 1-6.

DIRECTIONS: Questions 1 through 6 consist of descriptions of material to which a filing designation must be assigned.

Assume that the matters and oases described in the questions were referred for handling to a government legal office which has its files set up according to these file designations. The file designation consists of a number of characters and punctuation marks as described below.

The first character refers to agencies whose legal work is handled by this office. These agencies are numbered consecutively in the order in which they first submit a matter for attention, and are identified in an alphabetical card index. To date numbers have been assigned to agencies as follows:

Department of Correction 1
Police Department 2
Department of Traffic 3
Department of Consumer Affairs.. 4
Commission on Human Rights 5
Board of Elections 6
Department of Personnel.. 7
Board of Estimate 8

The second character is separated from the first character by a dash. The second character is the last digit of the year in which a particular lawsuit or matter is referred to the legal office.

The third character is separated from the second character by a colon and may consist of either of the following:

I. A sub-number assigned to each lawsuit to which the agency is a party. Lawsuits are numbered consecutively regardless of year. (Lawsuits are brought by or against agency heads rather than agencies themselves, but references are made to agencies for the purpose of simplification.)

or II. A capital letter assigned to each matter other than a lawsuit according to subject, the subject being identified in an alphabetical index. To date, letters have been assigned to subjects as follows:

Citizenship .... A
Discrimination .... B
Residence Requirements C
Civil Service Examinations .... D

Housing .... E
Gambling .... F
Freedom of Religion .... G

These referrals are numbered consecutively regardless of year. The first referral by a particular agency on citizenship, for example, would be designated A1, followed by A2, A3, etc.

If no reference is made in a question as to how many letters involving a certain subject or how many lawsuits have been referred by an agency, assume that it is the first.

For each question, choose the file designation which is MOST appropriate for filing the material described in the question.

1. In January, 2000, two candidates in a 1999 civil service examination for positions with the Department of Correction filed a suit against the Department of Personnel seeking to set aside an educational requirement for the title.
    The Department of Personnel immediately referred the law-suit to the legal office for handling.

    A. 1-9:1   B. 1-0:D1   C. 7-9:D1   D. 7-0:1

    1._____

2. In 2004, the Police Department made its sixth request for an opinion on whether an employee assignment proposed for 2005 could be considered discriminatory.

    A. 2-5:1-B6   B. 2-4:6   C. 2-4:1-B6   D. 2-4:B6

    2._____

3. In 2005, a lawsuit was brought by the Bay Island Action Committee against the Board of Estimate in which the plaintiff sought withdrawal of approval of housing for the elderly in the Bay Island area given by the Board in 2005.

    A. 8-3:1   B. 8-5:1   C. 8-3:B1   D. 8-5:E1

    3._____

4. In December 2004, community leaders asked the Police Department to ban outdoor meetings of a religious group on the grounds that the meetings were disrupting the area. Such meetings had been held from time to time during 2004. On January 31, 2005, the Police Department asked the government legal office for an opinion on whether granting this request would violate the worshippers' right to freedom of religion.

    A. 2-4:G-1   B. 2-5:G1   C. 2-5:B-1   D. 2-4:B1

    4._____

5. In 2004, a woman filed suit against the Board of Elections. She alleged that she had not been permitted to vote at her usual polling place in the 2003 election and had been told she was not registered there. She claimed that she had always voted there and that her record card had been lost. This was the fourth case of its type for this agency.

    A. 6-4:4   B. 6-3:C4   C. 3-4:6   D. 6-3:4

    5._____

6. A lawsuit was brought in 2001 by the Ace Pinball Machine Company against the Commissioner of Consumer Affairs. The lawsuit contested an ordinance which banned the use of pinball machines on the ground that they are gambling devices.
    This was the third lawsuit to which the Department of Consumer Affairs was a party.

    A. 4-1:1   B. 4-3:F1   C. 4-1:3   D. 3F-4:1

    6._____

7. You are instructed by your supervisor to type a statement that must be signed by the person making the statement and by three witnesses to the signature. The typed statement will take two pages and will leave no room for signatures if the normal margin is maintained at the bottom of the second page.
In this situation, the PREFERRED method is to type

    A. the signature lines below the normal margin on the second page
    B. nothing further and have the witnesses sign without a typed signature line
    C. the signature lines on a third page
    D. some of the text and the signature lines on a third page

7.____

8. Certain legal documents always begin with a statement of venue - that is, the county and state in which the document is executed. This is usually boxed with a parentheses or colons.
The one of the following documents that ALWAYS bears a statement of venue in a prominent position at its head is a(n)

    A. affidavit
    C. contract of sale
    B. memorandum of law
    D. will

8.____

9. You are requested to take stenographic notes and to transcribe the statements of a person under oath. The person has a heavy accent and speaks in ungrammatical and broken English.
When you are transcribing the testimony, of the following, the BEST thing for you to do is to

    A. transcribe the testimony exactly as spoken, making no grammatical changes
    B. make only the grammatical changes which would clarify the client's statements
    C. make all grammatical changes so that the testimony is in standard English form
    D. ask the client's permission before making any grammatical changes

9.____

10. When the material typed on a printed form does not fill the space provided, a Z-ruling is frequently drawn to fill up the unused space.
The MAIN purpose of this practice is to

    A. make the document more pleasing to the eye
    B. indicate that the preceding material is correct
    C. insure that the document is not altered
    D. show that the lawyer has read it

10.____

11. After you had typed an original and five copies of a certain document, some changes were made in ink on the original and were initialed by all the parties. The original was signed by all the parties, and the signatures were notarized.
Which of the following should *generally* be typed on the copies BEFORE filing the original and the copies? The inked changes

    A. but not the signatures, initials, or notarial data
    B. the signatures and the initials but not the notarial data
    C. and the notarial data but not the signatures or initials
    D. the signatures, the initials, and the notarial data

11.____

12. The first paragraph of a noncourt agreement *generally* contains all of the following EXCEPT the   12.____

    A.   specific terms of the agreement
    B.   date of the agreement
    C.   purpose of the agreement
    D.   names of the parties involved

13. When typing an answer in a court proceeding, the place where the word ANSWER should be typed on the first page of the document is   13.____

    A.   at the upper left-hand corner
    B.   below the index number and to the right of the box containing the names of the parties to the action
    C.   above the index number and to the right of the box containing the names of the parties to the action
    D.   to the left of the names of the attorneys for the defendant

14. Which one of the following statements BEST describes the legal document called an acknowledgment?
It is   14.____

    A.   an answer to an affidavit
    B.   a receipt issued by the court when a document is filed
    C.   proof of service of a summons
    D.   a declaration that a signature is valid

15. Suppose you typed the original and three carbon copies of a legal document which was dictated by an attorney in your office. He has already signed the original copy, and corrections have been made on all copies.
Regarding the carbon copies, which one of the following procedures is the PROPER one to follow?   15.____

    A.   Leave the signature line blank on the carbon copies
    B.   Ask the attorney to sign the carbon copies
    C.   Print or type the attorney's name on the signature line on the carbon copies
    D.   Sign your name to the carbon copies followed by the attorney's initials

16. Suppose your office is defending a particular person in a court action. This person comes to the office and asks to see some of the lawyer's working papers in his file. The lawyer assigned to the case is out of the office at the time.
You SHOULD   16.____

    A.   permit him to examine his entire file as long as he does not remove any materials from it
    B.   make an appointment for the caller to come back later when the lawyer will be there
    C.   ask him what working papers he wants to see and show him only those papers
    D.   tell him that he needs written permission from the lawyer in order to see any records

17. Suppose that you receive a phone call from an official who is annoyed about a letter from   17.____
     your office which she just received. The lawyer who dictated the letter is not in the office
     at the moment.
     Of the following, the BEST action for you to take is to

     A. explain that the lawyer is out but that you will ask the lawyer to return her call when
         he returns
     B. take down all of the details of her complaint and tell her that you will get back to her
         with an explanation
     C. refer to the proper file so that you can give her an explanation of the reasons for the
         letter over the phone
     D. make an appointment for her to stop by the office to speak with the lawyer

18. Suppose that you have taken dictation for an interoffice memorandum. You are asked to   18.____
     prepare it for distribution to four lawyers in your department whose names are given to
     you. You will type an original and four carbon copies. Which one of the following is COR-
     RECT with regard to the typing of the lawyers' names?
     The names of all of the lawyers should appear

     A. *only* on the original
     B. on the original and each copy should have the name of one lawyer
     C. on each of the copies but not on the original
     D. on the original and on all of the copies

19. Regarding the correct typing of punctuation, the GENERALLY accepted practice is that   19.____
     there should be

     A. two spaces after a semi-colon
     B. one space before an apostrophe used in the body of a word
     C. no space between parentheses and the matter enclosed
     D. one space before and after a hyphen

20. Suppose you have just completed typing an original and two copies of a letter   20.____
     requesting information. The original is to be signed by a lawyer in your office. The first
     copy is for the files, and the second is to be used as a reminder to follow up.
     The PROPER time to file the file copy of the letter is

     A. after the letter has been signed and corrections have been made on the copies
     B. before you take the letter to the lawyer for his signature
     C. after a follow-up letter has been sent
     D. after a response to the letter has been received

21. A secretary in a legal office has just typed a letter. She has typed the copy distribution   21.____
     notation on the copies to indicate *blind copy distribution*. This *blind copy* notation shows
     that

     A. copies of the letter are being sent to persons that the addressee does not know
     B. copies of the letter are being sent to other persons without the addressee's knowledge
     C. a copy of the letter will be enlarged for a legally blind person
     D. a copy of the letter is being given as an extra copy to the addressee

22. Suppose that one of the attorneys in your office dictates material to you without indicat-   22.___
ing punctuation. He has asked that you give him, as soon as possible, a single copy of a
rough draft to be triple-spaced so that he can make corrections.
Of the following, what is the BEST thing for you to do in this situation?

    A.   Assume that no punctuation is desired in the material
    B.   Insert the punctuation as you type the rough draft
    C.   Transcribe the material exactly as dictated, but attach a note to the attorney stating
       your suggested changes
    D.   Before you start to type the draft, tell the attorney you want to read back your notes
       so that he can indicate punctuation

23. When it is necessary to type a mailing notation such as CERTIFIED, REGISTERED, or   23.___
FEDEX on an envelope, the GENERALLY accepted place to type it is

    A.   directly above the address
    B.   in the area below where the stamp will be affixed
    C.   in the lower left-hand corner
    D.   in the upper left-hand corner

24. When taking a citation of a case in shorthand, which of the following should you write   24.___
FIRST if you are having difficulty keeping up with the dictation?

    A.   Volume and page number   B.   Title of volume
    C.   Name of plaintiff   D.   Name of defendant

25. All of the following abbreviations and their meanings are correctly paired EXCEPT   25.___

    A.   viz. - namely   B.   ibid. - refer
    C.   n.b. - note well   D.   q.v. - which see

KEY (CORRECT ANSWERS)

1.	D		11.	D
2.	D		12.	A
3.	B		13.	B
4.	B		14.	D
5.	A		15.	C
6.	C		16.	B
7.	D		17.	A
8.	A		18.	D
9.	A		19.	C
10.	C		20.	A

21.	B
22.	B
23.	B
24.	A
25.	B

EXAMINATION SECTION
TEST 1

DIRECTIONS: Each question or incomplete statement is followed by several suggested answers or completions. Select the one that BEST answers the question or completes the statement. *PRINT THE LETTER OF THE CORRECT ANSWER IN THE SPACE AT THE RIGHT.*

Questions 1-9.

DIRECTIONS: Questions 1 through 9 consist of sentences which may or may not be examples of good English usage. Consider grammar, punctuation, spelling, capitalization, awkwardness, etc. Examine each sentence, and then choose the correct statement about it from the four choices below it. If the English usage in the sentence given is better than it would be with any of the changes suggested in options B, C, and D, choose option A. Do not choose an option that will change the meaning of the sentence.

1. According to Judge Frank, the grocer's sons found guilty of assault and sentenced last Thursday.   1._____

     A. This is an example of acceptable writing.
     B. A comma should be placed after the word *sentenced.*
     C. The word *were* should be placed after *sons*
     D. The apostrophe in *grocer's* should be placed after the *s.*

2. The department heads assistant said that the stenographers should type duplicate copies of all contracts, leases, and bills.   2._____

     A. This is an example of acceptable writing.
     B. A comma should be placed before the word *contracts.*
     C. An apostrophe should be placed before the *s* in *heads.*
     D. Quotation marks should be placed before *the stenographers* and after *bills.*

3. The lawyers questioned the men to determine who was the true property owner?   3._____

     A. This is an example of acceptable writing.
     B. The phrase *questioned the men* should be changed to *asked the men questions.*
     C. The word *was* should be changed to *were.*
     D. The question mark should be changed to a period.

4. The terms stated in the present contract are more specific than those stated in the previous contract.   4._____

     A. This is an example of acceptable writing.
     B. The word *are* should be changed to *is.*
     C. The word *than* should be changed to *then.*
     D. The word *specific* should be changed to *specified.*

5. Of the lawyers considered, the one who argued more skillful was chosen for the job.   5._____

     A. This is an example of acceptable writing.
     B. The word *more* should be replaced by the word *most.*
     C. The word *skillful* should be replaced by the word *skillfully,*
     D. The word *chosen* should be replaced by the word *selected.*

6. Each of the states has a court of appeals; some states have circuit courts.   6._____

    A. This is an example of acceptable writing.
    B. The semi-colon should be changed to a comma.
    C. The word *has* should be changed to *have*.
    D. The word *some* should be capitalized.

7. The court trial has greatly effected the child's mental condition.   7._____

    A. This is an example of acceptable writing.
    B. The word *effected* should be changed to *affected*.
    C. The word *greatly* should be placed after *effected*.
    D. The apostrophe in *child's* should be placed after the *s*.

8. Last week, the petition signed by all the officers was sent to the Better Business Bureau.   8._____

    A. This is an example of acceptable writing.
    B. The phrase *last week* should be placed after *officers*.
    C. A comma should be placed after *petition*.
    D. The word *was* should be changed to *were*.

9. Mr. Farrell claims that he requested form A-12, and three booklets describing court pro-   9._____
    cedures.

    A. This is an example of acceptable writing.
    B. The word *that* should be eliminated.
    C. A colon should be placed after *requested*.
    D. The comma after *A-12* should be eliminated.

Questions 10-21.

DIRECTIONS: Questions 10 through 21 contain a word in capital letters followed by four sug-
              gested meanings of the word. For each question, choose the BEST meaning
              for the word in capital letters.

10. SIGNATORY - A   10._____

    A. lawyer who draws up a legal document
    B. document that must be signed by a judge
    C. person who signs a document
    D. true copy of a signature

11. RETAINER - A   11._____

    A. fee paid to a lawyer for his services
    B. document held by a third party
    C. court decision to send a prisoner back to custody pending trial
    D. legal requirement to keep certain types of files

12. BEQUEATH - To   12._____

    A. receive assistance from a charitable organization
    B. give personal property by will to another
    C. transfer real property from one person to another
    D. receive an inheritance upon the death of a relative

13. RATIFY - To

    A. approve and sanction   B. forego
    C. produce evidence   D. summarize

14. CODICIL - A

    A. document introduced in evidence in a civil action
    B. subsection of a law
    C. type of legal action that can be brought by a plaintiff
    D. supplement or an addition to a will

15. ALIAS

    A. Assumed name   B. In favor of
    C. Against   D. A writ

16. PROXY - A(n)

    A. phony document in a real estate transaction
    B. opinion by a judge of a civil court
    C. document containing appointment of an agent
    D. summons in a lawsuit

17. ALLEGED

    A. Innocent   B. Asserted
    C. Guilty   D. Called upon

18. EXECUTE - To

    A. complete a legal document by signing it
    B. set requirements
    C. render services to a duly elected executive of a municipality
    D. initiate legal action such as a lawsuit

19. NOTARY PUBLIC - A

    A. lawyer who is running for public office
    B. judge who hears minor cases
    C. public officer, one of whose functions is to administer oaths
    D. lawyer who gives free legal services to persons unable to pay

20. WAIVE - To

    A. disturb a calm state of affairs
    B. knowingly renounce a right or claim
    C. pardon someone for a minor fault
    D. purposely mislead a person during an investigation

21. ARRAIGN - To

    A. prevent an escape   B. defend a prisoner
    C. verify a document   D. accuse in a court of law

13.____ 14.____ 15.____ 16.____ 17.____ 18.____ 19.____ 20.____ 21.____

Questions 22-40.

DIRECTIONS: Questions 22 through 40 each consist of four words which may or may not be spelled correctly. If you find an error in
only one word, mark your answer A;
any two words, mark your answer B;
any three words, mark your answer C;
none of these words, mark your answer D.

22.	occurrence	Febuary	privilege	similiar	22.___
23.	separate	transferring	analyze	column	23.___
24.	develop	license	bankrupcy	abreviate	24.___
25.	subpoena	arguement	dissolution	foreclosure	25.___
26.	exaggerate	fundamental	significance	warrant	26.___
27.	citizen	endorsed	marraige	appraissal	27.___
28.	precedant	univercity	observence	preliminary	28.___
29.	stipulate	negligence	judgment	prominent	29.___
30.	judisial	whereas	release	guardian	30.___
31.	appeal	larcenny	transcrip	jurist	31.___
32.	petition	tenancy	agenda	insurance	32.___
33.	superfical	premise	morgaged	maintainance	33.___
34.	testamony	publically	installment	possessed	34.___
35.	escrow	decree	eviction	miscelaneous	35.___
36.	securitys	abeyance	adhere	corporate	36.___
37.	kaleidoscope	anesthesia	vermilion	tafetta	37.___
38.	congruant	barrenness	plebescite	vigilance	38.___
39.	picnicing	promisory	resevoir	omission	39.___
40.	supersede	banister	wholly	seize	40.___

KEY (CORRECT ANSWERS)

1.	C	11.	A	21.	D	31.	B
2.	C	12.	B	22.	B	32.	D
3.	D	13.	A	23.	D	33.	C
4.	A	14.	D	24.	B	34.	B
5.	C	15.	A	25.	A	35.	A
6.	A	16.	C	26.	D	36.	A
7.	B	17.	B	27.	B	37.	A
8.	A	18.	A	28.	C	38.	B
9.	D	19.	C	29.	D	39.	C
10.	C	20.	B	30.	A	40.	D

EXAMINATION SECTION
TEST 1

DIRECTIONS: Each question or incomplete statement is followed by several suggested answers or completions. Select the one that *BEST* answers the question or completes the statement. *PRINT THE LETTER OF THE CORRECT ANSWER IN THE SPACE AT THE RIGHT.*

Questions 1-5.

DIRECTIONS: Each question from 1 to 5 consists of a sentence with an underlined word. For each question, select the choice that is *CLOSEST* in meaning to the underlined word.

EXAMPLE

This division reviews the fiscal reports of the agency.
In this sentence the word *fiscal* means most nearly
   A. financial   B. critical   C. basic   D. personnel
The correct answer is A. "financial" because "financial" is closest to *fiscal*. Therefore, the answer is A.

1. Every good office worker needs basic skills.
   The word *basic* in this sentence means   1.____

   A. fundamental   B. advanced   C. unusual   D. outstanding

2. He turned out to be a good instructor.
   The word *instructor* in this sentence means   2.____

   A. student   B. worker   C. typist   D. teacher

3. The quantity of work in the office was under study.
   In this sentence, the word *quantity* means   3.____

   A. amount   B. flow   C. supervision   D. type

4. The morning was spent examining the time records.
   In this sentence, the word *examining* means   4.____

   A. distributing   B. collecting   C. checking   D. filing

5. The candidate filled in the proper spaces on the form.
   In this sentence, the word *proper* means   5.____

   A. blank   B. appropriate   C. many   D. remaining

Questions 6-8.

DIRECTIONS: You are to answer Questions 6 through 8 *SOLELY* on the basis of the information contained in the following paragraph:
   The increase in the number of public documents in the last two centuries closely matches the increase in population in the United States. The great number of public documents has become a serious threat to their usefulness. It is necessary to have programs which will reduce the number of public documents that are kept and which will, at the same time, assure keeping those that have value. Such programs need a great deal of thought to have any success.

6. According to the above paragraph, public documents may be less useful if 6.____

    A. the files are open to the public
    B. the record room is too small
    C. the copying machine is operated only during normal working hours
    D. too many records are being kept

7. According to the above paragraph, the growth of the population in the United States has matched the growth in the quantity of public documents for a period of, most nearly, 7.____

    A. 50 years   B. 100 years   C. 200 years   D. 300 years

8. According to the above paragraph, the increased number of public documents has made it necessary to 8.____

    A. find out which public documents are worth keeping
    B. reduce the great number of public documents by decreasing government services
    C. eliminate the copying of all original public documents
    D. avoid all new copying devices.

Questions 9-10.

DIRECTIONS: You are to answer Questions 9 and 10 *SOLELY* on the basis of the information contained in the following paragraph:

The work goals of an agency can best be reached if the employees understand and agree with these goals. One way to gain such understanding and agreement is for management to encourage and seriously consider suggestions from employees in the setting of agency goals.

9. On the basis of the paragraph above, the *BEST* way to achieve the work goals of an agency is to 9.____

    A. make certain that employees work as hard as possible
    B. study the organizational structure of the agency
    C. encourage employees to think seriously about the agency's problems
    D. stimulate employee understanding of the work goals

10. On the basis of the paragraph above, understanding and agreement with agency goals can be gained by 10.____

    A. allowing the employees to set agency goals
    B. reaching agency goals quickly
    C. legislative review of agency operations
    D. employee participation in setting agency goals

Questions 11-15.

DIRECTIONS: Each of Questions 11 through 15 consists of a group of four words. One word in each group is *INCORRECTLY* spelled. For each question, print the letter of the correct answer in the space at the right that is the same as the letter next to the word which is *INCORRECTLY* spelled.

EXAMPLE

    A. housing   B. certain   C. budgit   D. money

The word "budgit" is incorrectly spelled, because the correct spelling should be "budget." Therefore, the correct answer is C.

11.	A. sentince	B. bulletin	C. notice	D. definition	11.____
12.	A. appointment	B. exactly	C. typest	D. light	12.____
13.	A. penalty	B. suparvise	C. consider	D. division	13.____
14.	A. schedule	B. accurate	C. corect	D. simple	14.____
15.	A. suggestion	B. installed	C. proper	D. agincy	15.____

Questions 16-20.

DIRECTIONS: Each question from 16 through 20 consists of a sentence which may be
   A. incorrect because of bad word usage, or
   B. incorrect because of bad punctuation, or
   C. incorrect because of bad spelling, or
   D. correct

Read each sentence carefully. Then print in the proper space at the right A, B, C, or D, according to the answer you choose from the four choices listed above. There is only one type of error in each incorrect sentence. If there is no error, the sentence is correct.

EXAMPLE

George Washington was the father of his contry.

This sentence is incorrect because of bad spelling ("contry" instead of "country"). Therefore, the answer is C.

16. The assignment was completed in record time but the payroll for it has not yet been pre-parid.   16.____

17. The operator, on the other hand, is willing to learn me how to use the mimeograph.   17.____

18. She is the prettiest of the three sisters.   18.____

19. She doesn't know; if the mail has arrived.   19.____

20. The doorknob of the office door is broke.   20.____

21. A clerk can process a form in 15 minutes. How many forms can that clerk process in six hours?   21.____

   A. 10   B. 21   C. 24   D. 90

22. An office staff consists of 120 people. Sixty of them have been assigned to a special project. Of the remaining staff, 20 answer the mail, 10 handle phone calls, and the rest operate the office machines. The number of people operating the office machines is   22.____

   A. 20   B. 30   C. 40   D. 45

23. An office worker received 65 applications but on the first day had to return 26 of them for being incomplete and on the second day 25 had to be returned for being incomplete. How many applications did <u>not</u> have to be returned?   23.____

   A. 10   B. 12   C. 14   D. 16

24. An office worker answered 63 phone calls in one day and 91 phone calls the next day. For these 2 days, what was the average number of phone calls he answered per day?

    A. 77   B. 28   C. 82   D. 93

24.____

25. An office worker processed 12 vouchers of $8.75 each, 3 vouchers of $3.68 each, and 2 vouchers of $1.29 each. The total dollar amount of these vouchers is

    A. $116.04   B. $117.52   C. $118.62   D. $119.04

25.____

KEY (CORRECT ANSWERS)

1.	A		11.	A
2.	D		12.	C
3.	A		13.	B
4.	C		14.	C
5.	B		15.	D
6.	D		16.	C
7.	C		17.	A
8.	A		18.	D
9.	D		19.	B
10.	D		20.	A

21.	C
22.	B
23.	C
24.	A
25.	C

TEST 2

DIRECTIONS: Each question or incomplete statement is followed by several suggested answers or completions. Select the one that *BEST* answers the question or completes the statement. *PRINT THE LETTER OF THE CORRECT ANSWER IN THE SPACE AT THE RIGHT.*

Questions 1-5.

DIRECTIONS: Each question from 1 to 5 lists four names. The names may or may not be exactly the same. Compare the names in each question and mark your answer as follows:

Mark your answer A if all the names are different
Mark your answer B if only two names are exactly the same
Mark your answer C if only three names are exactly the same
Mark your answer D if all four names are exactly the same

EXAMPLE

Jensen, Alfred E.
Jensen, Alfred E.
Jensan, Alfred E.
Jensen, Fred E.

Since the name Jensen, Alfred E. appears twice and is exactly the same in both places, the correct answer is B.

1. Riviera, Pedro S.
   Rivers, Pedro S.
   Riviera, Pedro N.
   Riviera, Juan S.

   1.____

2. Guider, Albert
   Guidar, Albert
   Giuder, Alfred
   Guider, Albert

   2.____

3. Blum, Rona
   Blum, Rona
   Blum, Rona
   Blum, Rona

   3.____

4. Raugh, John
   Raugh, James
   Raughe, John
   Raugh, John

   4.____

5. Katz, Stanley
   Katz, Stanley
   Katze, Stanley
   Katz, Stanley

   5.____

Questions 6-10.

DIRECTIONS: Each Question 6 through 10 consists of numbers or letters in Columns I and II. For each question, compare each line of Column I with its corresponding line in Column II and decide how many lines in Column I are *EXACTLY* the same as their corresponding lines in Column II. In your answer space, mark your answer as follows:

Mark your answer A if only *ONE* line in Column I is exactly the same as its corresponding line in Column II

Mark your answer B if only *TWO* lines in Column I are exactly the same as their corresponding lines in Column II

Mark your answer C if only *THREE* lines in Column I are exactly the same as their corresponding lines in Column II

Mark your answer D if all *FOUR* lines in Column I are exactly the same as their corresponding lines in Column II

EXAMPLE

Column I	Column II
1776	1776
1865	1865
1945	1945
1976	1978

Only three lines in Column I are exactly the same as their corresponding lines in Column II. Therefore, the correct answer is C.

	Column I	Column II	
6.	5653	5653	6.___
	8727	8728	
	ZPSS	ZPSS	
	4952	9453	
7.	PNJP	PNPJ	7.___
	NJPJ	NJPJ	
	JNPN	JNPN	
	PNJP	PNPJ	
8.	effe	eFfe	8.___
	uWvw	uWvw	
	KpGj	KpGg	
	vmnv	vmnv	
9.	5232	5232	9.___
	PfrC	PfrN	
	zssz	zzss	
	rwwr	rwww	
10.	czws	czws	10.___
	cecc	cece	
	thrm	thrm	
	lwtz	lwtz	

Questions 11-15.

DIRECTIONS: Questions 11 through 15 have lines of letters and numbers. Each letter should be matched with its number in accordance with the following table:

Letter	F	R	C	A	W	L	E	N	B	T
Matching Number	0	1	2	3	4	5	6	7	8	9

From the table you can determine that the letter F has the matching number 0 below it, the letter R has the matching number 1 below it, etc.

For each question, compare each line of letters and numbers carefully to see if each letter has its correct matching number. If all the letters and numbers are matched correctly in
none of the lines of the question, mark your answer A
only one of the lines of the question, mark your answer B
only two of the lines of the question, mark your answer C
all three lines of the question, mark your answer D

EXAMPLE

WBCR	4826
TLBF	9580
ATNE	3986

There is a mistake in the first line because the letter R should have its matching number 1 instead of the number 6.

The second line is correct because each letter shown has the correct matching number.

There is a mistake in the third line because the letter N should have the matching number 7 instead of the number 8,

Since all the letters and numbers are matched correctly in only one of the lines in the sample, the correct answer is B.

11.	EBCT	6829		11.____
	ATWR	3961		
	NLBW	7584		
12.	RNCT	1729		12.____
	LNCR	5728		
	WAEB	5368		
13.	NTWB	7948		13.____
	RABL	1385		
	TAEF	9360		
14.	LWRB	5417		14.____
	RLWN	1647		
	CBWA	2843		
15.	ABTC	3792		15.____
	WCER	5261		
	AWCN	3417		

16. Your job often brings you into contact with the public. Of the following, it would be *MOST*   16.____
desirable to explain the reasons for official actions to people coming into your office for
assistance because such explanations

    A.   help build greater understanding between the public and your agency
    B.   help build greater self-confidence in city employees
    C.   convince the public that nothing they do can upset a city employee
    D.   show the public that city employees are intelligent

17. Assume that you strongly dislike one of your co-workers.   17.____
You should *FIRST*

    A.   discuss your feeling with the co-worker
    B.   demand a transfer to another office
    C.   suggest to your supervisor that the co-worker should be observed carefully
    D.   try to figure out the reason for this dislike before you say or do anything

18. An office worker who has problems accepting authority is *MOST* likely to find it difficult to   18.____

    A.   obey rules   B.   understand people
    C.   assist other employees   D.   follow complex instructions

19. The employees in your office have taken a dislike to one person and frequently annoy   19.____
her. Your supervisor *should*

    A.   transfer this person to another unit at the first opportunity
    B.   try to find out the reason for the staff's attitude before doing anything about it
    C.   threaten to transfer the first person observed bothering this person
    D.   ignore the situation

20. Assume that your supervisor has asked a worker in your office to get a copy of a report   20.____
out of the files. You notice the worker has accidentally pulled out the wrong report.
Of the following, the *BEST* way for you to handle this situation is to tell

    A.   the worker about all the difficulties that will result from this error
    B.   the worker about her mistake in a nice way
    C.   the worker to ignore this error
    D.   your supervisor that this worker needs more training in how to use the files

21. Filing systems differ in their efficiency. Which of the following is the *BEST* way to evaluate   21.____
the efficiency of a filing system?
The

    A.   number of times used per day
    B.   amount of material that is received each day for filing
    C.   amount of time it takes to locate material
    D.   type of locking system used

22. In planning ahead so that a sufficient amount of general office supplies is always avail-   22.____
able, it would be *LEAST* important to find out the

    A.   current office supply needs of the staff
    B.   amount of office supplies used last year
    C.   days and times that office supplies can be ordered
    D.   agency goals and objectives

23. The *MAIN* reason for establishing routine office work procedures is that once a routine is established   23.____

    A. work need not be checked for accuracy
    B. all steps in the routine will take an equal amount of time to perform
    C. each time the job is repeated it will take less time to perform
    D. each step in the routine will not have to be planned all over again each time

24. When an office machine centrally located in an agency must be shut down for repairs, the bureaus and divisions using this machine should be informed of the   24.____

    A. expected length of time before the machine will be in operation again
    B. estimated cost of repairs
    C. efforts being made to avoid future repairs
    D. type of new equipment which the agency may buy in the future to replace the machine being repaired

25. If the day's work is properly scheduled, the *MOST* important result would be that the   25.____

    A. supervisor will not have to do much supervision
    B. employee will know what to do next
    C. employee will show greater initiative
    D. job will become routine

KEY (CORRECT ANSWERS)

1.	A		11.	C
2.	B		12.	B
3.	D		13.	D
4.	B		14.	B
5.	C		15.	A
6.	B		16.	A
7.	B		17.	D
8.	B		18.	A
9.	A		19.	B
10.	C		20.	B

21.	C
22.	D
23.	D
24.	A
25.	B

EXAMINATION SECTION
TEST 1

DIRECTIONS: Each question or incomplete statement is followed by several suggested answers or completions. Select the one that BEST answers the question or completes the statement. *PRINT THE LETTER OF THE CORRECT ANSWER IN THE SPACE AT THE RIGHT.*

Questions 1-10.

WORD MEANING

DIRECTIONS: Each question from 1 to 10 contains a word in capitals followed by four suggested meanings of the word. For each question, choose the best meaning. *PRINT THE LETTER OF THE CORRECT ANSWER IN THE SPACE AT THE RIGHT.*

1. ACCURATE   1._____
   A. correct   B. useful   C. afraid   D. careless

2. ALTER   2._____
   A. copy   B. change   C. report   D. agree

3. DOCUMENT   3._____
   A. outline   B. agreement   C. blueprint   D. record

4. INDICATE   4._____
   A. listen   B. show   C. guess   D. try

5. INVENTORY   5._____
   A. custom   B. discovery   C. warning   D. list

6. ISSUE   6._____
   A. annoy   B. use up   C. give out   D. gain

7. NOTIFY   7._____
   A. inform   B. promise   C. approve   D. strengthen

8. ROUTINE   8._____
   A. path   B. mistake   C. habit   D. journey

9. TERMINATE   9._____
   A. rest   B. start   C. deny   D. end

10. TRANSMIT   10._____
    A. put in   B. send   C. stop   D. go across

Questions 11-15.

READING COMPREHENSION

DIRECTIONS: Questions 11 through 15 test how well you understand what you read. It will be
necessary for you to read carefully because your answers to these questions
should be based ONLY on the information given in the following paragraphs.

*The recipient gains an impression of a typewritten letter before he begins to read the
message. Pastors which provide for a good first impression include margins and spacing that
are visually pleasing, formal parts of the letter which are correctly placed according to the
style of the letter, copy which is free of obvious erasures and over-strikes, and transcript that
is even and clear. The problem for the typist is that of how to produce that first, positive
impression of her work.*

*There are several general rules which a typist can follow when she wishes to prepare a
properly spaced letter on a sheet of letter-head. Ordinarily, the width of a letter should not be
less than four inches nor more than six inches. The side margins should also have a desirable relation to the bottom margin and the space between the letterhead and the body of the
letter. Usually the most appealing arrangement is when the side margins are even and the
bottom margin is slightly wider than the side margins. In some offices, however, standard line
length is used for all business letters, and the secretary then varies the spacing between the
date line and the inside address according to the length of the letter.*

11.   The BEST title for the above paragraphs would be: 11._____

    A.   Writing Office Letters
    B.   Making Good First Impressions
    C.   Judging Well-Typed Letters
    D.   Good Placing and Spacing for Office Letters

12.   According to the above paragraphs, which of the following might be considered the way   12._____
in which people very quickly judge the quality of work which has been typed? By

    A.   measuring the margins to see if they are correct
    B.   looking at the spacing and cleanliness of the typescript
    C.   scanning the body of the letter for meaning
    D.   reading the date line and address for errors

13.   What, according to the above paragraphs, would be definitely UNDESIRABLE as the   13._____
average line length of a typed letter?

    A.   4"   B.   5"   C.   6"   D.   7"

14.   According to the above paragraphs, when the line length is kept standard, the secretary   14._____

    A.   does not have to vary the spacing at all since this also is standard
    B.   adjusts the spacing between the date line and inside address for different lengths
of letters
    C.   uses the longest line as a guideline for spacing between the date line and inside
address
    D.   varies the number of spaces between the lines

15. According to the above paragraphs, side margins are MOST pleasing when they 15.____

    A. are even and somewhat smaller than the bottom margin
    B. are slightly wider than the bottom margin
    C. vary with the length of the letter
    D. are figured independently from the letterhead and the body of the letter

Questions 16-20.

CODING

DIRECTIONS:

Name of Applicant	H A N G S B R U K E
Test Code	c o m p l e x i t y
File Number	0 1 2 3 4 5 6 7 8 9

Assume that each of the above capital letters is the first letter of the name of an Applicant, that the small letter directly beneath each capital letter is the test code for the Applicant, and that the number directly beneath each code letter is the file number for the Applicant.

In each of the following Questions 16 through 20, the test code letters and the file numbers in Columns 2 and 3 should correspond to the capital letters in Column 1. For each question, look at each column carefully and mark your answer as follows:

    If there is an error only in Column 2, mark your answer A.
    If there is an error only in Column 3, mark your answer B.
    If there is an error in both Columns 2 and 3, mark your answer C.
    If both Columns 2 and 3 are correct, mark your answer D.

The following sample question is given to help you understand the procedure.

SAMPLE QUESTION

Column 1	Column 2	Column 3
AKEHN	otyci	18902

In Column 2, the final test code letter *i*. should be *m*. Column 3 is correctly coded to Column 1. Since there is an error only in Column 2, the answer is A.

	Column 1	Column 2	Column 3	
16.	NEKKU	mytti	29987	16.____
17.	KRAEB	txyle	86095	17.____
18.	ENAUK	ymoit	92178	18.____
19.	REANA	xeomo	69121	19.____
20.	EKHSE	ytcxy	97049	20.____

Questions 21-30.

ARITHMETICAL REASONING

21. If a secretary answered 28 phone calls and typed the addresses for 112 credit state-   21._____
ments in one morning, what is the ratio of phone calls answered to credit statements
typed for that period of time?

    A. 1:4   B. 1:7   C. 2:3   D. 3:5

22. According to a suggested filing system, no more than 10 folders should be filed behind   22._____
any one file guide and from 15 to 25 file guides should be used in each file drawer for
easy finding and filing.
The maximum number of folders that a five-drawer file cabinet can hold to allow easy
finding and filing is

    A. 550   B. 750   C. 1,100   D. 1,250

23. An employee had a starting salary of $25,804. He received a salary increase at the end   23._____
of each year, and at the end of the seventh year his salary was $33,476.
What was his average annual increase in salary over these seven years?

    A. $1,020   B. $1,076   C. $1,096   D. $1,144

24. The 55 typists and 28 senior clerks in a certain city agency were paid a total of   24._____
$1,943,200 in salaries last year.
If the average annual salary of a typist was $22,400 the average annual salary of a
senior clerk was

    A. $25,400   B. $26,600   C. $26,800   D. $27,000

25. A typist has been given a three page report to type. She has finished typing the first two   25._____
pages. The first page has 283 words, and the second page has 366 words.
If the total report consists of 954 words, how many words will she have to type on the
third page of the report?

    A. 202   B. 287   C. 305   D. 313

26. In one day, Clerk A processed 30% more forms than Clerk B, and Clerk C processed li   26._____
times as many forms as Clerk A. If Clerk B processed 40 forms, how many more forms
were processed by Clerk C than Clerk B?

    A. 12   B. 13   C. 21   D. 25

27. A clerk who earns a gross salary of $452 every two weeks has the following deductions   27._____
taken from her paycheck:
15% for City, State, Federal taxes; 2 1/2% for Social Security; $1.30 for health insur-
ance; and $6.00 for union dues. The amount of her take-home pay is

    A. $256.20   B. $312.40   C. $331.60   D. $365.60

28. In 2005, a city agency spent $2,000 to buy pencils at a cost of $5.00 a dozen.   28._____
If the agency used 3/4 of these pencils in 2005 and used the same number of pencils
in 2006, how many more pencils did it have to buy to have enough pencils for all of
2006?

    A. 1,200   B. 2,400   C. 3,600   D. 4,800

29. A clerk who worked in Agency X earned the following salaries: $20,140 the first year,$21,000 the second year, and $21,920 the third year. Another clerk who worked in Agency Y for three years earned $21,100 a year for two years and $21,448 the third year. The difference between the average salaries received by both clerks over a three-year period is   29.____

    A. $196   B. $204   C. $348   D. $564

30. An employee who works over 40 hours in any week receives overtime payment for the extra hours at time and one-half (1 1/2 times) his hourly rate of pay. An employee who earns $13.60 an hour works a total of 45 hours during a certain week.
His total pay for that week would be   30.____

    A. $564.40   B. $612.00   C. $646.00   D. $812.00

Questions 31-35.

RELATED INFORMATION

31. To tell a newly-employed clerk to fill a top drawer of a four-drawer cabinet with heavy folders which will be often used and to keep lower drawers only partly filled is   31.____

    A. *good,* because a tall person would have to bend unnecessarily if he had to use a lower drawer
    B. *bad,* because the file cabinet may tip over when the top drawer is opened
    C. *good,* because it is the most easily reachable drawer for the average person
    D. *bad,* because a person bending down at another drawer may accidentally bang his head on the bottom of the drawer when he straightens up

32. If a senior typist or senior clerk has requisitioned a *ream* of paper in order to duplicate a single page office announcement, how many announcements can be printed from the one package of paper?   32.____

    A. 200   B. 500   C. 700   D. 1,000

33. Your supervisor has asked you to locate a telephone number for an attorney named Jones, whose office is located at 311 Broadway, and whose name is not already listed in your files.
The BEST method for finding the number would be for you to   33.____

    A. call the information operator and have her get it for you
    B. look in the alphabetical directory (white pages) under the name Jones at 311 Broadway
    C. refer to the heading Attorney in the yellow pages for the name Jones at 311 Broadway
    D. ask your supervisor who referred her to Mr. Jones, then call that person for the number

34. An example of material that should NOT be sent by first class mail is a   34.____

    A. email copy of a letter   B. post card
    C. business reply card   D. large catalogue

35. In the operations of a government agency, a voucher is ORDINARILY used to   35.____

     A. refer someone to the agency for a position or assignment
     B. certify that an agency's records of financial trans-actions are accurate
     C. order payment from agency funds of a stated amount to an individual
     D. enter a statement of official opinion in the records of the agency

Questions 36-40.

ENGLISH USAGE

DIRECTIONS: Each question from 36 through 40 contains a sentence. Read each sentence carefully to decide whether it is correct. Then, in the space at the right, mark your answer:

     (A) if the sentence is incorrect because of bad grammar or sentence structure

     (B) if the sentence is incorrect because of bad punctuation

     (C) if the sentence is incorrect because of bad capitalization

     (D) if the sentence is correct

     Each incorrect sentence has only one type of error. Consider a sentence correct if it has no errors, although there may be other correct ways of saying the same thing.

     SAMPLE QUESTION I: One of our clerks were promoted yesterday.

     The subject of this sentence is *one,* so the verb should be *was promoted* instead of *were promoted.* Since the sentence is incorrect because of bad grammar, the answer to Sample Question I is (A).

     SAMPLE QUESTION II: Between you and me, I would prefer not going there.

     Since this sentence is correct, the answer to Sample Question II is (D).

36. The National alliance of Businessmen is trying to persuade private businesses to hire   36.____
youth in the summertime.

37. The supervisor who is on vacation, is in charge of processing vouchers.   37.____

38. The activity of the committee at its conferences is always stimulating.   38.____

39. After checking the addresses again, the letters went to the mailroom.   39.____

40. The director, as well as the employees, are interested in sharing the dividends.   40.____

Questions 41-45.

FILING

DIRECTIONS: Each question from 41 through 45 contains four names. For each question, choose the name that should be FIRST if the four names are to be arranged in alphabeti-cal order in accordance with the Rules for Alphabetical Filing given below. Read these rules carefully. Then, for each question, indicate in the space at the right the letter before the name that should be FIRST in alphabet-ical order.

RULES FOR ALPHABETICAL FILING

Names of People

(1) The names of people are filed in strict alphabetical order, first according to the last name, then according to first name or initial, and finally according to middle name or initial. FOR EXAMPLE: George Allen comes before Edward Bell, and Leonard P. Reston comes before Lucille B. Reston.

(2) When last names are the same, FOR EXAMPLE, A. Green and Agnes Green, the one with the initial comes before the one with the name written out when the first initials are identi-cal.

(3) When first and last names are alike and the middle name is given, FOR EXAMPLE, John David Doe and John Devoe Doe, the names should be filed in the alphabetical order of the middle names.

(4) When first and last names are the same, a name without a middle initial comes before one with a middle name or initial. FOR EXAMPLE, John Doe comes before both John A. Doe and John Alan Doe.

(5) When first and last names are the same, a name with a middle initial comes before one with a middle name beginning with the same initial. FOR EXAMPLE: Jack R. Hertz comes before Jack Richard Hertz.

(6) Prefixes such as De, O', Mac, Mc, and Van are filed as written and are treated as part of the names to which they are connected. FOR EXAMPLE: Robert O'Dea is filed before David Olsen.

(7) Abbreviated names are treated as if they were spelled out. FOR EXAMPLE: Chas. is filed as Charles and Thos. is filed as Thomas.

(8) Titles and designations such as Dr., Mr., and Prof, are disregarded in filing.

Names of Organizations

(1) The names of business organizations are filed according to the order in which each word in the name appears. When an organization name bears the name of a person, it is filed according to the rules for filing names of people as given above. FOR EXAMPLE: William Smith Service Co. comes before Television Distributors, Inc.

(2) *Where bureau, board, office, or department appears as the first part of the title of a governmental agency, that agency should be filed under the word in the title expressing the chief function of the agency. FOR EXAMPLE: Bureau of the Budget would be filed as if written Budget, (Bureau of the). The Department of Personnel would be filed as if written Personnel, (Department of).*

(3) *When the following words are part of an organization, they are disregarded: the, of, and.*

(4) *When there are numbers in a name, they are treated as if they were spelled out. FOR EXAMPLE: 10th Street Bootery is filed as Tenth Street Bootery.*

<u>SAMPLE QUESTION:</u>

A. Jane Earl   (2)
B. James A. Earle   (4)
C. James Earl   (1)
D. J. Earle   (3)

The numbers in parentheses show the proper alphabetical order in which these names should be filed. Since the name that should be filed FIRST is James Earl, the answer to the Sample Question is (C).

41. A. Majorca Leather Goods   41._____
     B. Robert Maiorca and Sons
     C. Maintenance Management Corp.
     D. Majestic Carpet Mills

42. A. Municipal Telephone Service   42._____
     B. Municipal Reference Library
     C. Municipal Credit Union
     D. Municipal Broadcasting System

43. A. Robert B. Pierce   B. R. Bruce Pierce   43._____
     C. Ronald Pierce   D. Robert Bruce Pierce

44. A. Four Seasons Sports Club   B. 14th. St. Shopping Center   44._____
     C. Forty Thieves Restaurant   D. 42nd St. Theaters

45. A. Franco Franceschini   B. Amos Franchini   45._____
     C. Sandra Franceschia   D. Lilie Franchinesca

Questions 46-50.

SPELLING

DIRECTIONS: In each question, one of the words is misspelled. Select the letter of the misspelled word. *PRINT THE LETTER OF THE CORRECT ANSWER IN THE SPACE AT THE RIGHT.*

46. A. option   B. extradite   46._____
     C. comparitive   D. jealousy

47. A. handicaped   B. assurance   47._____
     C. sympathy   D. speech

48. A. recommend B. carraige 48.____
     C. disapprove D. independent

49. A. ingenuity B. tenet (opinion) 49.____
     C. uncanny D. intrigueing

50. A. arduous B. hideous 50.____
     C. iervant D. companies

KEY (CORRECT ANSWERS)

1.	A	11.	D	21.	A	31.	B	41.	C
2.	B	12.	B	22.	D	32.	B	42.	D
3.	D	13.	D	23.	C	33.	C	43.	B
4.	B	14.	B	24.	A	34.	D	44.	D
5.	D	15.	A	25.	C	35.	C	45.	C
6.	C	16.	B	26.	D	36.	C	46.	C
7.	A	17.	C	27.	D	37.	B	47.	A
8.	C	18.	D	28.	B	38.	D	48.	B
9.	D	19.	A	29.	A	39.	A	49.	D
10.	B	20.	C	30.	C	40.	A	50.	C'

EXAMINATION SECTION
TEST 1

DIRECTIONS: Each question or incomplete statement is followed by several suggested
answers or completions. Select the one that BEST answers the question or
completes the statement. *PRINT THE LETTER OF THE CORRECT ANSWER
IN THE SPACE AT THE RIGHT.*

1. A push-button telephone with six buttons, one of which is a *hold* button, is often used   1.____
   when more than one outside line is needed.
   If you are talking on one line of this type of telephone when another call comes in, what
   is the procedure to follow if you want to answer the second call but keep the first call on
   the line? Push the

   A. *hold* button at the same time as you push the *pickup* button of the ringing line
   B. *hold* button and then push the *pickup* button of the ringing line
   C. *pickup* button of the ringing line and then push the *hold* button
   D. *pickup* button of the ringing line and push the *hold* button when you return to the
       original line

2. Suppose that you are asked to prepare a petty cash statement for March. The original   2.____
   and one copy are to go to the personnel office. One copy is to go to the fiscal office, and
   another copy is to go to your supervisor. The last copy is for your files.
   In preparing the statement and the copies, how many sheets of copy paper should you
   use?

   A. 3   B. 4   C. 5   D. 8

3. Which one of the following is the LEAST important advantage of putting the subject of a   3.____
   letter in the heading to the right of the address?
   It

   A. makes filing of the copy easier
   B. makes more space available in the body of the letter
   C. simplifies distribution of letters
   D. simplifies determination of the subject of the letter

4. Of the following, the MOST efficient way to put 100 copies of a one-page letter into 9 1/2”   4.____
   x 4 1/8” envelopes for mailing is to fold _____ into an envelope.

   A. each letter and insert it immediately after folding
   B. each letter separately until all 100 are folded; then insert each one
   C. the 100 letters two at a time, then separate them and insert each one
   D. two letters together, slip them apart, and insert each one

5. When preparing papers for filing, it is NOT desirable to   5.____

   A. smooth papers that are wrinkled
   B. use paper clips to keep related papers together in the files
   C. arrange the papers in the order in which they will be filed
   D. mend torn papers with cellophane tape

6. Of the following, the BEST reason for a clerical unit to have its own duplicating machine is that the unit   6._____

    A. uses many forms which it must reproduce internally
    B. must make two copies of each piece of incoming mail for a special file
    C. must make seven copies of each piece of outgoing mail
    D. must type 200 envelopes each month for distribution to the same offices

7. Several offices use the same photocopying machine.   7._____
If each office must pay its share of the cost of running this machine, the BEST way of determining how much of this cost should be charged to each of these offices is to

    A. determine the monthly number of photocopies made by each office
    B. determine the monthly number of originals submitted for photocopying by each office
    C. determine the number of times per day each office uses the photocopy machine
    D. divide the total cost of running the photocopy machine by the total number of offices using the machine

8. Which one of the following would it be BEST to use to indicate that a file folder has been removed from the files for temporary use in another office?   8._____
A(n)

    A. cross-reference card   B. tickler file marker
    C. aperture card   D. out guide

9. Which one of the following is the MOST important objective of filing?   9._____

    A. Giving a secretary something to do in her spare time
    B. Making it possible to locate information quickly
    C. Providing a place to store unneeded documents
    D. Keeping extra papers from accumulating on workers' desks

10. If a check has been made out for an incorrect amount, the BEST action for the writer of the check to take is to   10._____

    A. erase the original amount and enter the correct amount
    B. cross out the original amount with a single line and enter the correct amount above it
    C. black out the original amount so that it cannot be read and enter the correct amount above it
    D. write a new check

11. Which one of the following BEST describes the usual arrangement of a tickler file?   11._____

    A. Alphabetical   B. Chronological
    C. Numerical   D. Geographical

12. Which one of the following is the LEAST desirable filing practice?   12._____

    A. Using staples to keep papers together
    B. Filing all material without regard to date
    C. Keeping a record of all materials removed from the files
    D. Writing filing instructions on each paper prior to filing

13. Assume that one of your duties is to keep records of the office supplies used by your unit   13.____
for the purpose of ordering new supplies when the old supplies run out. The information
that will be of MOST help in letting you know when to reorder supplies is the

    A. quantity issued   B. quantity received
    C. quantity on hand   D. stock number

Questions 14-19.

DIRECTIONS: Questions 14 through 19 consist of sets of names and addresses. In each
question, the name and address in Column II should be an exact copy of the
name and address in Column I. If there is:
    a mistake *only* in the name, mark your answer A;
    a mistake *only* in the address, mark your answer B;
    a mistake in *both* name and address, mark your answer C;
    no mistake in *either* name or address, mark your answer D.

SAMPLE QUESTION

Column I	Column II
Michael Filbert	Michael Filbert
456 Reade Street	645 Reade Street
New York, N.Y. 10013	New York, N.Y. 10013

Since there is a mistake only in the address (the street number should be 456
instead of 645), the answer to the sample question is B.

COLUMN I	COLUMN II	
14. Esta Wong 141 West 68 St. New York, N.Y. 10023	Esta Wang 141 West 68 St. New York, N.Y. 10023	14.____
15. Dr. Alberto Grosso 3475 12th Avenue Brooklyn, N.Y. 11218	Dr. Alberto Grosso 3475 12th Avenue Brooklyn, N.Y. 11218	15.____
16. Mrs. Ruth Bortlas 482 Theresa Ct. Far Rockaway, N.Y. 11691	Ms. Ruth Bortlas 482 Theresa Ct. Far Rockaway, N.Y. 11169	16.____
17. Mr. and Mrs. Howard Fox 2301 Sedgwick Ave. Bronx, N.Y. 10468	Mr. and Mrs. Howard Fox 231 Sedgwick Ave. Bronx, N.Y. 10468	17.____
18. Miss Marjorie Black 223 East 23 Street New York, N.Y. 10010	Miss Margorie Black 223 East 23 Street New York, N.Y. 10010	18.____
19. Michelle Herman 806 Valley Rd. Old Tappan, N.J. 07675	Michelle Hermann 806 Valley Dr. Old Tappan, N.J. 07675	19.____

Questions 20-25.

DIRECTIONS: Questions 20 through 25 are to be answered SOLELY on the basis of the information in the following passage.

Basic to every office is the need for proper lighting. Inadequate lighting is a familiar cause of fatigue and serves to create a somewhat dismal atmosphere in the office. One requirement of proper lighting is that it be of an appropriate intensity. Intensity is measured in foot-candles. According to the Illuminating Engineering Society of New York, for casual seeing tasks such as in reception rooms, inactive file rooms, and other service areas, it is recommended that the amount of light be 30 foot-candles. For ordinary seeing tasks such as reading and work in active file rooms and in mail rooms, the recommended lighting is 100 foot-candles. For very difficult seeing tasks such as accounting, transcribing, and business machine use, the recommended lighting is 150 foot-candles.

Lighting intensity is only one requirement. Shadows and glare are to be avoided. For example, the larger the proportion of a ceiling filled with lighting units, the more glare-free and comfortable the lighting will be. Natural lighting from windows is not too dependable because on dark wintry days, windows yield little usable light, and on sunny, summer afternoons, the glare from windows may be very distracting. Desks should not face the windows. Finally, the main lighting source ought to be overhead and to the left of the user.

20. According to the above passage, insufficient light in the office may cause   20._____

    A. glare
    B. shadows
    C. tiredness
    D. distraction

21. Based on the above passage, which of the following must be considered when planning   21._____
lighting arrangements?
The

    A. amount of natural light present
    B. amount of work to be done
    C. level of difficulty of work to be done
    D. type of activity to be carried out

22. It can be inferred from the above passage that a well-coordinated lighting scheme is   22._____
LIKELY to result in

    A. greater employee productivity
    B. elimination of light reflection
    C. lower lighting cost
    D. more use of natural light

23. Of the following, the BEST title for the above passage is   23._____

    A. Characteristics of Light
    B. Light Measurement Devices
    C. Factors to Consider When Planning Lighting Systems
    D. Comfort vs. Cost When Devising Lighting Arrangements

24. According to the above passage, a foot-candle is a measurement of the   24._____
    - A. number of bulbs used
    - B. strength of the light
    - C. contrast between glare and shadow
    - D. proportion of the ceiling filled with lighting units

25. According to the above passage, the number of foot-candles of light that would be   25._____
    needed to copy figures onto a payroll is _____ foot-candles.
    - A. less than 30
    - C. 100
    - B. 30
    - D. 150

KEY (CORRECT ANSWERS)

1.	B		11.	B
2.	B		12.	B
3.	B		13.	C
4.	A		14.	A
5.	B		15.	D
6.	A		16.	C
7.	A		17.	B
8.	D		18.	A
9.	B		19.	C
10.	D		20.	C

21.	D
22.	A
23.	C
24.	B
25.	D

TEST 2

DIRECTIONS: Each question or incomplete statement is followed by several suggested answers or completions. Select the one that BEST answers the question or completes the statement. *PRINT THE LETTER OF THE CORRECT ANSWER IN THE SPACE AT THE RIGHT.*

1. Assume that a supervisor has three subordinates who perform clerical tasks. One of the employees retires and is replaced by someone who is transferred from another unit in the agency. The transferred employee tells the supervisor that she has worked as a clerical employee for two years and understands clerical operations quite well. The supervisor then assigns the transferred employee to a desk, tells the employee to begin working, and returns to his own desk.
The supervisor's action in this situation is   1.____

   A. *proper;* experienced clerical employees do not require training when they are transferred to new assignments
   B. *improper;* before the supervisor returns to his desk, he should tell the other two subordinates to watch the transferred employee perform the work
   C. *proper;* if the transferred employee makes any mistakes, she will bring them to the supervisor's attention
   D. *improper;* the supervisor should find out what clerical tasks the transferred employee has performed and give her instruction in those which are new or different

2. Assume that you are falling behind in completing your work assignments and you believe that your workload is too heavy.
Of the following, the BEST course of action for you to take FIRST is to   2.____

   A. discuss the problem with your supervisor
   B. decide which of your assignments can be postponed
   C. try to get some of your co-workers to help you out
   D. plan to take some of the work home with you in order to catch up

3. Suppose that one of the clerks under your supervision is filling in monthly personnel forms. She asks you to explain a particular personnel regulation which is related to various items on the forms. You are not thoroughly familiar with the regulation.
Of the following responses you may make, the one which will gain the MOST respect from the clerk and which is generally the MOST advisable is to   3.____

   A. tell the clerk to do the best she can and that you will check her work later
   B. inform the clerk that you are not sure of a correct explanation but suggest a procedure for her to follow
   C. give the clerk a suitable interpretation so that she will think you are familiar with all regulations
   D. tell the clerk that you will have to read the regulation more thoroughly before you can give her an explanation

4. Charging out records until a specified due date, with prompt follow-up if they are not returned, is a   4.____

A. *good* idea; it may prevent the records from being kept needlessly on someone's desk for long periods of time
B. *good* idea; it will indicate the extent of your authority to other departments
C. *poor* idea; the person borrowing the material may make an error because of the pressure put upon him to return the records
D. *poor* idea; other departments will feel that you do not trust them with the records and they will be resentful

Questions 5-9.

DIRECTIONS: Questions 5 through 9 consist of three lines of code letters and numbers. The numbers on each line should correspond with the code letters on the same line in accordance with the table below.

Code Letter	P	L	I	J	B	0	H	U	C	G
Corresponding Number	0	1	2	3	4	5	6	7	8	9

On some of the lines, an error exists in the coding. Compare the letters and numbers in each question carefully. If you find an error or errors on
only *one* of the lines in the question, mark your answer A;
any *two* lines in the question, mark your answer B;
all *three* lines in the question, mark your answer C;
none of the lines in the question, mark your answer D.

SAMPLE QUESTION

JHOILCP   3652180
BICLGUP   4286970
UCIBHLJ   5824613

In the above sample, the first line is correct since each code letter listed has the correct corresponding number. On the second line, an error exists because code letter L should have the number 1 instead of the number 6. On the third line, an error exists because the code letter U should have the number 7 instead of the number 5. Since there are errors on two of the three lines, the correct answer is B.

5. BULJCIP   4713920   5._____
    HIGPOUL   6290571
    OCUHJBI   5876342

6. CUBLOIJ   8741023   6._____
    LCLGCLB   1818914
    JPUHIOC   3076158

7. OIJGCBPO   52398405   7._____
    UHPBLIOP   76041250
    CLUIPGPC   81720908

8. BPCOUOJI   40875732   8._____
    UOHCIPLB   75682014
    GLHUUCBJ   92677843

9. HOIOHJLH   65256361   9._____
    IOJJHHBP   25536640
    OJHBJOPI   53642502

Questions 10-13.

DIRECTIONS: Questions 10 through 13 are to be answered SOLELY on the basis of the infor-
               mation given in the following passage.

The mental attitude of the employee toward safety is exceedingly important in preventing
accidents. All efforts designed to keep safety on the employee's mind and to keep accident
prevention a live subject in the office will help substantially in a safety program. Although it
may seem strange, it is common for people to be careless. Therefore, safety education is a
continuous process.

Safety rules should be explained, and the reasons for their rigid enforcement should be
given to employees. Telling employees to be careful or giving similar general safety warnings
and slogans is probably of little value. Employees should be informed of basic safety funda-
mentals. This can be done through staff meetings, informal suggestions to employees, mov-
ies, and safety instruction cards. Safety instruction cards provide the employees with specific
suggestions about safety and serve as a series of timely reminders helping to keep safety on
the minds of employees. Pictures, posters, and cartoon sketches on bulletin boards that are
located in areas continually used by employees arouse the employees' interest in safety. It is
usually good to supplement this type of safety promotion with intensive individual follow-up.

10. The above passage implies that the LEAST effective of the following safety measures is   10._____

     A.   rigid enforcement of safety rules
     B.   getting employees to think in terms of safety
     C.   elimination of unsafe conditions in the office
     D.   telling employees to stay alert at all times

11. The reason given by the passage for maintaining ongoing safety education is that   11._____

     A.   people are often careless
     B.   office tasks are often dangerous
     C.   the value of safety slogans increases with repetition
     D.   safety rules change frequently

12. Which one of the following safety aids is MOST likely to be preferred by the passage?   12._____
     A

     A.   cartoon of a man tripping over a carton and yelling, *Keep aisles clear!*
     B.   poster with a large number one and a caption saying, *Safety First*
     C.   photograph of a very neatly arranged office
     D.   large sign with the word *THINK* in capital letters

13. Of the following, the BEST title for the above passage is   13.____

    A. Basic Safety Fundamentals
    B. Enforcing Safety Among Careless Employees
    C. Attitudes Toward Safety
    D. Making Employees Aware of Safety

Questions 14-21.

DIRECTIONS: Questions 14 through 21 are to be answered SOLELY on the basis of the information and the chart given below.

    The following chart shows expenses in five selected categories for a one-year period,
expressed as percentages of these same expenses during the previous year. The chart com-
pares two different offices. In Office T (represented by ▨▨▨), a cost reduction program

has been tested for the past year. The other office, Office Q (represented by ▨▨▨), served
as a control, in that no special effort was made' to reduce costs during the past year.

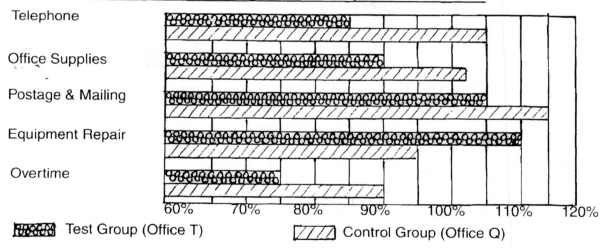

RESULTS OF OFFICE COST REDUCTION PROGRAM
Expenses of Test and Control Groups for 2009
Expressed as Percentages of Same Expenses for 2008

14. In Office T, which category of expense showed the greatest percentage REDUCTION   14.____
    from 2008 to 2009?

    A. Telephone   B. Office Supplies
    C. Postage & Mailing   D. Overtime

15. In which expense category did Office T show the BEST results in percentage terms   15.____
    when compared to Office Q?

    A. Telephone   B. Office Supplies
    C. Postage & Mailing   D. Overtime

16. According to the above chart, the cost reduction program was LEAST effective for the   16.____
    expense category of

    A. Office Supplies   B. Postage & Mailing
    C. Equipment Repair   D. Overtime

17. Office T's telephone costs went down during 2009 by approximately how many percent-   17.____
    age points?

    A. 15   B. 20   C. 85   D. 105

18. Which of the following changes occurred in expenses for Office Supplies in Office Q in   18.____
    the year 2009 as compared with the year 2008?
    They

    A. increased by more than 100%
    B. remained the same
    C. decreased by a few percentage points
    D. increased by a few percentage points

19. For which of the following expense categories do the results in Office T and the results in   19.____
    Office Q differ MOST NEARLY by 10 percentage points?

    A. Telephone   B. Postage & Mailing
    C. Equipment Repair   D. Overtime

20. In which expense category did Office Q's costs show the GREATEST percentage   20.____
    increase in 2009?

    A. Telephone   B. Office Supplies
    C. Postage & Mailing   D. Equipment Repair

21. In Office T, by approximately what percentage did overtime expense change during the   21.____
    past year?
    It

    A. increased by 15%   B. increased by 75%
    C. decreased by 10%   D. decreased by 25%

22. In a particular agency, there were 160 accidents in 2007. Of these accidents, 75% were   22.____
    due to unsafe acts and the rest were due to unsafe conditions. In the following year, a
    special safety program was established. The number of accidents in 2009 due to unsafe
    acts was reduced to 35% of what it had been in 2007.
    How many accidents due to unsafe acts were there in 2009?

    A. 20   B. 36   C. 42   D. 56

23. At the end of every month, the petty cash fund of Agency A is reimbursed for payments   23.____
    made from the fund during the month. During the month of February, the amounts paid
    from the fund were entered on receipts as follows: 10 bus fares of 35¢ each and one taxi
    fare of $3.50.
    At the end of the month, the money left in the fund was in the following denominations:
    15 one dollar bills, 4 quarters, 10 dimes, and 20 nickels.
    If the petty cash fund is reduced by 20% for the following month, how much money will
    there be available in the petty cash fund for March?

    A. $11.00   B. $20.00   C. $21.50   D. $25.00

24. The one of the following records which it would be MOST advisable to keep in alphabetical order is a

    A. continuous listing of phone messages, including time and caller, for your supervisor
    B. listing of individuals currently employed by your agency in a particular title
    C. record of purchases paid for by the petty cash fund
    D. dated record of employees who have borrowed material from the files in your office

24.____

25. Assume that you have been asked to copy by hand a column of numbers with two decimal places from one record to another. Each number consists of three, four, and five digits.
In order to copy them quickly and accurately, you should copy

    A. each number exactly, making sure that the column of digits farthest to the right is in a straight line and all other columns are lined up
    B. the column of digits farthest to the right and then copy the next column of digits moving from right to left
    C. the column of digits farthest to the left and then copy the next column of digits moving from left to right
    D. the digits to the right of each decimal point and then copy the digits to the left of each decimal point

25.____

―――――

KEY (CORRECT ANSWERS)

1.	D		11.	A
2.	A		12.	A
3.	D		13.	D
4.	A		14.	D
5.	A		15.	A
6.	C		16.	C
7.	D		17.	A
8.	B		18.	D
9.	C		19.	B
10.	D		20.	C

21.	D
22.	C
23.	B
24.	B
25.	A

―――――

EXAMINATION SECTION
TEST 1

DIRECTIONS: Each question or incomplete statement is followed by several suggested answers or completions. Select the one that BEST answers the question or completes the statement. *PRINT THE LETTER OF THE CORRECT ANSWER IN THE SPACE AT THE RIGHT.*

Questions 1-25

Each sentence in questions 1-25 includes four words with letters over them. One of these words has been typed incorrectly. Indicate the misspelled word by printing the letter in the space at the right.

1.   1.____

          A   B
If the administrator attempts to withold information,
                     C
there is a good likelihood that there will be serious
       D
repercussions.

2.   2.____

        A   B   C
He condescended to apologize, but we felt that a beligerent
                         D
person should not occupy an influential position.

3.   3.____

          A   B   C
Despite the sporadic delinquent payments of his indebted-
                   D
ness, Mr. Johnson has been an exemplery customer.

4.   4.____

          A   B
He was appreciative of the support he consistantly
   C   D
acquired, but he felt that he had waited an inordinate
length of time for it.

5.   5.____

          A   B
Undeniably they benefited from the establishment of a
   C   D
receivership, but the question or statutary limitations
remained unresolved.

6.   6._____

           A
Mr. Smith profered his hand as an indication that he
                B   C
considered it a viable contract, but Mr. Nelson alluded
              D
to the fact that his colleagues had not been consulted.

7.   7._____

                           A   B
The treatments were beneficial according to the optomo-
                    C   D
trists, and the consensus was that minimal improvement
could be expected.

8.   8._____

           A
Her frivalous manner was unbecoming because the air of
      B   C   D
solemnity at the cemetery was pervasive.

9.   9._____

            A
The clandestine meetings were designed to make the two
      B   C
adversaries more amicible, but they served only to
                 D
intensify their emnity.

10.   10._____

                   A
Do you think that his innovative ideas and financial
      B   C   D
acumen will help stabalize the fluctuations of the stock
market?

11.   11._____

                 A
In order to keep a perpetual inventory, you will have to
                    B   C   D
keep an uninterrupted surveillance of all the miscellaneous
stock.

12.   12._____

                 A
She used the art of pursuasion on the children because
                    B   C   D
she found that caustic remarks had no perceptible effect
on their behavior.

13.

          A   B

His sacreligious outbursts offended his constituents , and

               C   D

he was summarily removed from office by the City Council.

13._____

14.

          A   B

They exhorted the contestants to greater efforts, but the

         C

exhorbitant costs in terms of energy expended resulted in

         D

a feeling of lethargy.

14._____

15.

         A   B

Since he was knowledgable about illicit drugs, he was

         C   D

served with a subpoena to appear for the prosecution.

15._____

16.

         A   B

In spite of his lucid statements, they denigrated his

         C   D

report and decided it should be succintly paraphrased.

16._____

17.

         A   B

The discussion was not germane to the contraversy, but

     C   D

the indicted man's insistence on further talk was allowed.

17._____

18.

         A   B

The legislators were enervated by the distances they had

      C   D

traveled during the election year to fulfil their speaking

engagements.

18._____

19.

         A   B   C

The plaintiffs' attornies charged the defendant in the

         D

case with felonious assault.

19._____

20.   20._____

         A   B
It is symptomatic of the times that we try to placate
                                    C
all, but a proposal for new forms of disciplinery action
              D
was promulgated by the staff.

21.   21._____

         A
A worrysome situation has developed as a result of the
      B   C
assessment that absenteeism is increasing despite our
         D
conscientious efforts.

22.   22._____

         A   B
I concurred with the credit manager that it was practi-
                              C
cable to charge purchases on a biennial basis, and the
                         D
company agreed to adhear to this policy.

23.   23._____

                    A   B   C
The pastor was chagrined and embarassed by the irreverent
                              D
conduct of one of his parishioners.

24.   24._____

         A   B   C
His inate seriousness was belied by his flippant
D
demeanor.

25.   25._____

         A   B   C
It was exceedingly regrettable that the excessive number
         D
of challanges in the court delayed the start of the
trial.

Questions 26-45.

In each of the following sentences, numbered 26-45, <u>there may be an error.</u> Indicate the appropriate correction by printing the corresponding letter in the space at the right. If the sentence is correct as is, indicate this by printing the corresponding letter in the space at the right. <u>Unnecessary changes will be considered incorrect.</u>

26. In that building there seemed to be representatives of Teachers College, the Veterans Bureau, and the Businessmen's Association.

    A.   Teacher's College   B.   Veteran's Bureau
    C.   Businessmens Association   D.   correct as is

26.____

27. In his travels, he visited St. Paul, San Francisco, Springfield, Ohio, and Washington, D.C..

    A.   Ohio and   B.   Saint Paul
    C.   Washington, D.C.   D.   correct as is

27.____

28. As a result of their purchasing a controlling interest in the syndicate, it was well-known that the Bureau of Labor Statistics' calculations would be unimportant.

    A.   of them purchasing   B.   well known
    C.   Statistics   D.   correct as is

28.____

29. Walter Scott, Jr.'s, attempt to emulate his father's success was doomed to failure.

    A.   Junior's,   B.   Scott's, Jr.,
    C.   Scott, Jr.'s attempt   D.   correct as is

29.____

30. About B.C. 250 the Romans invaded Great Britain, and remains of their highly developed civilization can still be seen.

    A.   250 B.C.   B.   Britain and
    C.   highly-developed   D.   correct as is

30.____

31. The two boss's sons visited the children's department.

    A.   bosses   B.   bosses'
    C.   childrens'   D.   correct as is

31.____

32. Miss Amex not only approved the report, but also decided that it needed no revision.

    A.   report; but   B.   report but
    C.   report. But   D.   correct as is

32.____

33. Here's brain food in a jiffy--economical too!

    A.   economical too!   B.   'brain food'
    C.   jiffy-economical   D.   correct as is

33.____

34. She said, "He likes the "Gatsby Look" very much."

    A.   said "He   B.   "he
    C.   'Gatsby Look'   D.   correct as is

34.____

35. We anticipate that we will be able to visit them briefly in Los Angeles on Wednesday after   35.____
a 5-day visit.

    A.   Wednes-   B.   5-day
    C.   briefly   D.   correct as is

36. She passed all her tests, and, she now has a good position.   36.____

    A.   tests, and she   B.   past
    C.   tests;   D.   correct as is

37. The billing clerk said, "I will send the bill today"; however, that was a week ago, and it   37.____
hasn't arrived yet!

    A.   today;"   B.   today,"
    C.   ago and   D.   correct as is

38. "She types at more-than-average speed," Miss Smith said, "but I feel that it is a result of   38.____
marvelous concentration and self control on her part."

    A.   more than average   B.   "But
    C.   self-control   D.   correct as is

39. The state of Alaska, the largest state in the union, is also the northernmost state.   39.____

    A.   Union   B.   Northernmost State
    C.   State of Alaska   D.   correct as is

40. The memoirs of Ex-President Nixon, will sell more copies than <u>Six Crises</u>, the book he   40.____
wrote in the 60's.

    A.   Six Crises   B.   ex-President
    C.   60s   D.   correct as is

41. He spoke on his favorite topic, "Why We Will Win." (How could *I* stop him?)   41.____

    A.   Win".   B.   him?).
    C.   him)?   D.   correct as is

42. "All any insurance policy is, is a contract for services," said my insurance agent, Mr. New-   42.____
ton.

    A.   Insurance Policy   B.   Insurance Agent
    C.   policy is is a   D.   correct as is

43. Inasmuch as the price list has not been up dated, we should send it to the printer.   43.____

    A.   In as much   B.   updated
    C.   pricelist   D.   correct as is

44. We feel that "Our know-how" is responsible for the improvement in technical develop-   44.____
ments.

    A.   "our   B.   know how
    C.   that,   D.   correct as is

45. Did Cortez conquer the Incas? the Aztecs? the South American Indians?   45.____

    A.   Incas, the Aztecs, the South American Indians?
    B.   Incas; the Aztecs; the South American Indians?
    C.   south American Indians?
    D.   correct as is

Questions 46-70.

In the article which follows, certain words or groups of words are underlined and numbered. The underlined word or group of words may be incorrect because they present an error in grammer, usage, sentence structure, capitalization, diction, or punctuation. For each numbered word or group of words, there is an identically numbered question consisting of four choices based only on the underlined portion. For each question numbered 46-70, indicate the best choice by print-ing the corresponding letter in the space at the right. Unnecessary changes will be considered incorrect.

TIGERS VIE FOR CITY CHAMPIONSHIP

In their second year of varsity football, the North Side
Tigers have gained a shot at the city championship. Last Saturday
in the play-offs, the Tigers defeated the Western High School
                                    46
Cowboys, thus eliminated that team from contention. Most of the
credit for the team's improvement must go to Joe Harris, the
                                    47
coach. To play as well as they do now, the coach must have given
the team superior instruction. There is no doubt that, if a
          48
coach is effective, his influence is over many young minds.
        With this major victory behind them, the Tigers can now look
          49
forward to meet the defending champions, the Revere Minutemen, in
the finals.
                            50
        The win over the Cowboys was due to North Side's supremacy
in the air. The Tigers' players have the advantage of strength
          51
and of being speedy. Our sterling quarterback, Butch Carter, a
          52
master of the long pass, used these kind of passes to bedevil the
                                            53
boys from Western. As a matter of fact, if the Tigers would have
used the passing offense earlier in the game, the score would have
been more one sided. Butch, by the way, our all-around senior
student, has already been tapped for bigger things. Having the
                                            54
highest marks in his class, Barton College has offered him a
scholarship.
        The team's defense is another story. During the last few
                                            55
weeks, neither the linebackers nor the safety man have shown
sufficient ability to contain their opponents' running game. In
                            56
the city final, the defensive unit's failing to complete it's
assignments may lead to disaster. However, the coach said that
                            57
this unit not only has been cooperative, but also the coach
praised their eagerness to learn. He also said that this team
        58

has <u>not and never will give up</u>. This kind of spirit is contag-
                    59
ious, <u>therefore</u> I predict that the Tigers will win because I have
                    60
<u>affection and full confidence in</u> the team.
        One of the happy surprises this season is Peter Yisko, our
            61
punter. Peter <u>is</u> in the United States for only two years. When
he was in grammar school in the old country, it was not necessary
                    62
for him <u>to have studied</u> hard. Now, he depends on the football
                                    63
team to help him with his English. Everybody <u>but the team mascot</u>
and I have been pressed into service. Peter was ineligible last
                64
year when he <u>learned that he would only obtain half</u> of the credits
he had completed in Europe. Nevertheless, he attended occasional
practice sessions, but he soon found out that, if one wants to be
                    65
a successful player, <u>you</u> must realize that regular practice is
required. In fact, if a team is to be successful, it is necessary
                66
that everyone <u>be</u> present for all practice sessions. "The life of
                                67
a football player," says Peter, "is better than <u>a scholar</u>."
Facing the Minutemen, the Tigers will meet their most
                                        68
formidable opposition yet. This team <u>is not only gaining a bad</u>
reputation but also indulging in illegal practices on the field.
                    69
They <u>can't hardly object to us being</u> technical about penalties
under these circumstances. As far as the Minutemen are concerned,
                    70
a <u>victory will taste sweet like a victory should</u>.

46.   A.   , that eliminated that team   46. _____
      B.   and they were eliminated
      C.   and eliminated them
      D.   correct as is

47.   A.   To make them play as well as they do   47. _____
      B.   Having played so well
      C.   After they played so well
      D.   correct as is

48.   A.   if coaches are effective; they have influence over   48. _____
      B.   to be effective, a coach influences
      C.   if a coach is effective, he influences
      D.   correct as is

49.

    A.   to meet with   B.   to meeting
    C.   to a meeting of   D.   correct as is

           49._____

50.

    A.   because of   B.   on account *of*
    C.   motivated by   D.   correct as is

           50._____

51.

    A.   operating swiftly   B.   speed
    C.   running speedily   D.   correct as is

           51._____

52.

    A.   these kinds of pass   B.   this kind of passes
    C.   this kind of pass   D.   correct as is

           52._____

53.

    A.   would be used   B.   had used
    C.   were using   D.   correct as is

           53._____

54.   A.   he was offered a scholarship by Barton College.
       B.   Barton College offered a scholarship to him.
       C.   a scholarship was offered him by Barton College.
       D.   correct as is

           54._____

55.

    A.   had shown   B.   were showing
    C.   has shown   D.   correct as is

           55._____

56.   A.   the defensive unit failing to complete its assignment
       B.   the defensive unit's failing to complete its assignment
       C.   the defensive unit failing to complete it's assignment
       D.   correct as is

           56._____

57.   A.   has been not only cooperative, but also eager to learn
       B.   has not only been cooperative, but also shows eagerness to learn
       C.   has been not only cooperative, but also they were eager to learn
       D.   correct as is

           57._____

58.   A.   has not given up and never will
       B.   has not and never would give up
       C.   has not given up and never will give up
       D.   correct as is

           58._____

59.

    A.   .Therefore   B.   : therefore
    C.   --therefore   D.   correct as is

           59._____

60. A. full confidence and affection for
     B. affection for and full confidence in
     C. affection and full confidence concerning
     D. correct as is

60. ____

61.

     A. is living   B. was living
     C. has been   D. correct as is

61. ____

62.

     A. to study   B. to be studying
     C. to have been studying D. correct as is

62. ____

63. A. but the team mascot and me has
     B. but the team mascot and myself has
     C. but the team mascot and me have
     D. correct as is

63. ____

64. A. only learned that he would obtain hall
     B. learned that he would obtain only half
     C. learned that he only would obtain half
     D. correct as is

64. ____

65.

     A. a person   B. everyone
     C. one   D. correct as is

65. ____

66.

     A. is   B. will be
     C. shall be   D. correct as is

66. ____

67.

     A. to be a scholar   B. being a scholar
     C. that of a scholar   D. correct as is

67. ____

68. A. not only is gaining a bad reputation
     B. is gaining not only a bad reputation
     C. is not gaining only a bad reputation
     D. correct as is

68. ____

69. A. can hardly object to us being
     B. can hardly object to our being
     C. can't hardly object to our being
     D. correct as is

69. ____

70. A. victory will taste sweet like it should.
     B. victory will taste sweetly as it should taste.
     C. victory will taste sweet as a victory should.
     D. correct as is

70. ____

KEY (CORRECT ANSWERS

1. B	16. C	31. B	46. C	61. C
2. C	17. B	32. B	47. A	62. A
3. D	18. D	33. D	48. C	63. A
4. B	19. B	34. C	49. B	64. B
5. D	20. C	35. B	50. A	65. C
6. A	21. A	36. A	51. B	66. D
7. B	22. D	37. D	52. C	67. C
8. A	23. B	38. D	53. B	68. D
9. C	24. A	39. A	54. D	69. A
10. C	25. D	40. B	55. C	70. C
11. D	26. D	41. D	56. B	
12. A	27. C	42. D	57. A	
13. A	28. B	43. B	58. B	
14. C	29. D	44. A	59. A	
15. A	30. A	45. D	60. B	

———

DIRECTIONS: Each question or incomplete statement is followed by several suggested answers or completions. Select the one that BEST answers the question or completes the statement. *PRINT THE LETTER OF THE CORRECT ANSWER IN THE SPACE AT THE RIGHT.*

Questions 1-25.

DIRECTIONS: In each of Questions 1 through 25, select the lettered word or phrase which means MOST NEARLY the same as the capitalized word.

1. INTERROGATE   1.____
  A. question   B. arrest   C. search   D. rebuff

2. PERVERSE   2.____
  A. manageable   B. poetic
  C. contrary   D. patient

3. ADVOCATE   3.____
  A. champion   B. employ
  C. select   D. advise

4. APPARENT   4.____
  A. desirable   B. clear
  C. partial   D. possible

5. INSINUATE   5.____
  A. survey   B. strengthen
  C. suggest   D. insist

6. MOMENTOUS   6.____
  A. important   B. immediate   C. delayed   D. short

7. AUXILIARY   7.____
  A. exciting   B. assisting   C. upsetting   D. available

8. ADMONISH   8.____
  A. praise   B. increase   C. warn   D. polish

9. ANTICIPATE   9.____
  A. agree   B. expect   C. conceal   D. approve

10. APPREHEND   10.____
  A. confuse   B. sentence   C. release   D. seize

11. CLEMENCY   11.____
  A. silence   B. freedom   C. mercy   D. severity

12. THWART   12.____
  A. enrage   B. strike   C. choke   D. block

13. RELINQUISH   13.____
    A. stretch   B. give up   C. weaken   D. flee from

14. CURTAIL   14.____
    A. stop   B. reduce   C. repair   D. insult

15. INACCESSIBLE   15.____
    A. obstinate   B. unreachable
    C. unreasonable   D. puzzling

16. PERTINENT   16.____
    A. related   B. saucy   C. durable   D. impatient

17. INTIMIDATE   17.____
    A. encourage   B. hunt   C. beat   D. frighten

18. INTEGRITY   18.____
    A. honesty   B. wisdom
    C. understanding   D. persistence

19. UTILIZE   19.____
    A. use   B. manufacture
    C. help   D. include

20. SUPPLEMENT   20.____
    A. regulate   B. demand   C. add   D. answer

21. INDISPENSABLE   21.____
    A. essential   B. neglected
    C. truthful   D. unnecessary

22. ATTAIN   22.____
    A. introduce   B. spoil   C. achieve   D. study

23. PRECEDE   23.____
    A. break away   B. go ahead
    C. begin   D. come before

24. HAZARD   24.____
    A. penalty   B. adventure   C. handicap   D. danger

25. DETRIMENTAL   25.____
    A. uncertain   B. harmful   C. fierce   D. horrible

KEY (CORRECT ANSWERS)

1. A	6. A	11. C	16. A	21. A
2. C	7. B	12. D	17. D	22. C
3. A	8. C	13. B	18. A	23. D
4. B	9. B	14. B	19. A	24. D
5. C	10. D	15. B	20. C	25. B

TEST 2

Questions 1-20.

1. IMPLY   1.____
   A. agree to   B. hint at   C. laugh at
   D. mimic   E. reduce

2. APPRAISAL   2.____
   A. allowance   B. composition   C. prohibition
   D. quantity   E. valuation

3. DISBURSE   3.____
   A. approve   B. expend   C. prevent
   D. relay   E. restrict

4. POSTERITY   4.____
   A. back payment   B. current procedure   C. final effort
   D. future generations E. rare specimen

5. PUNCTUAL   5.____
   A. clear   B. honest   C. polite
   D. prompt   E. prudent

6. PRECARIOUS   6.____
   A. abundant   B. alarmed   C. cautious
   D. insecure   E. placid

7. FOSTER   7.____
   A. delegate   B. demote   C. encourage
   D. plead   E. surround

8. PINNACLE   8.____
   A. center   B. crisis   C. outcome
   D. peak   E. personification

9. COMPONENT   9.____
   A. flattery   B. opposite   C. part
   D. revision   E. trend

10. SOLICIT   10.____
   A. ask   B. prohibit   C. promise
   D. revoke   E. surprise

11. LIAISON   11.___
    A. asset   B. coordination   C. difference
    D. policy   E. procedure

12. ALLEGE   12.___
    A. assert   B. break   C. irritate
    D. reduce   E. wait

13. INFILTRATION   13.___
    A. consumption   B. disposal   C. enforcement
    D. penetration   E. seizure

14. SALVAGE   14.___
    A. announce   B. combine   C. prolong
    D. save   E. try

15. MOTIVE   15.___
    A. attack   B. favor   C. incentive
    D. patience   E. tribute

16. PROVOKE   16.___
    A. adjust   B. incite   C. leave
    D. obtain   E. practice

17. SURGE   17.___
    A. branch   B. contract   C. revenge
    D. rush   E. want

18. MAGNIFY   18.___
    A. attract   B. demand   C. generate
    D. increase   E. puzzle

19. PREPONDERANCE   19.___
    A. decision   B. judgment   C. outweighing
    D. submission   E. warning

20. ABATE   20.___
    A. assist   B. coerce   C. diminish
    D. indulge   E. trade

Questions 21-30.

DIRECTIONS: In each of Questions 21 through 30, select the lettered word or phrase which
               means MOST NEARLY, the same as, or the opposite of, the capitalized word.

21. VINDICTIVE   21.___
    A. centrifugal   B. forgiving   C. molten
    D. tedious   E. vivacious

22. SCOPE   22.___
    A. compact   B. detriment   C. facsimile
    D. potable   E. range

23. HINDER   23.___
    A. amplify   B. aver   C. method
    D. observe   E. retard

24. IRATE   24.___
    A. adhere   B. angry   C. authentic
    D. peremptory   E. vacillate

25. APATHY   25.___
    A. accessory   B. availability   C. fervor
    D. pacify   E. stride

26. LUCRATIVE   26.___
    A. effective   B. imperfect   C. injurious
    D. timely   E. worthless

27. DIVERSITY   27.___
    A. convection   B. slip   C. temerity
    D. uniformity   E. viscosity

28. OVERT   28.___
    A. laugh   B. lighter   C. orifice
    D. quay   E. sly

29. SPORADIC   29.___
    A. divide   B. incumbrance   C. livid
    D. occasional   E. original

30. PREVARICATE   30.___
    A. hesitate   B. increase   C. lie
    D. procrastinate   E. reject

———

KEY (CORRECT ANSWERS)

1.	B	11.	B	21.	B
2.	E	12.	A	22.	E
3.	B	13.	D	23.	E
4.	D	14.	D	24.	B
5.	D	15.	C	25.	C
6.	D	16.	B	26.	E
7.	C	17.	D	27.	D
8.	D	18.	D	28.	E
9.	C	19.	C	29.	D
10.	A	20.	C	30.	C

———

TEST 3

Each question or incomplete statement is followed by several suggested answers or completions. Select the one that BEST answers the question or completes the statement. *PRINT THE LETTER OF THE CORRECT ANSWER IN THE SPACE AT THE RIGHT.*

Questions 1-30.

DIRECTIONS: In each of Questions 1 through 30, select the lettered word which means MOST NEARLY the same as the capitalized word.

1. AVARICE   1.____
   A. flight   B. greed   C. pride   D. thrift

2. PREDATORY   2.____
   A. offensive   B. plundering
   C. previous   D. timeless

3. VINDICATE   3.____
   A. clear   B. conquer   C. correct   D. illustrate

4. INVETERATE   4.____
   A. backward   B. erect   C. habitual   D. lucky

5. DISCERN   5.____
   A. describe   B. fabricate   C. recognize   D. seek

6. COMPLACENT   6.____
   A. indulgent   B. listless   C. overjoyed   D. satisfied

7. ILLICIT   7.____
   A. insecure   B. unclear   C. unlawful   D. unlimited

8. PROCRASTINATE   8.____
   A. declare   B. multiply   C. postpone   D. steal

9. IMPASSIVE   9.____
   A. calm   B. frustrated
   C. thoughtful   D. unhappy

10. AMICABLE   10.____
   A. cheerful   B. flexible
   C. friendly   D. poised

11. FEASIBLE   11.____
   A. breakable   B. easy
   C. likeable   D. practicable

12. INNOCUOUS   12.____
   A. harmless   B. insecure
   C. insincere   D. unfavorable

13. OSTENSIBLE   13.____
- A. apparent
- B. hesitant
- C. reluctant
- D. showy

14. INDOMITABLE   14.____
- A. excessive
- B. unconquerable
- C. unreasonable
- D. unthinkable

15. CRAVEN   15.____
- A. cowardly
- B. hidden
- C. miserly
- D. needed

16. ALLAY   16.____
- A. discuss
- B. quiet
- C. refine
- D. remove

17. ALLUDE   17.____
- A. denounce
- B. refer
- C. state
- D. support

18. NEGLIGENCE   18.____
- A. carelessness
- B. denial
- C. objection
- D. refusal

19. AMEND   19.____
- A. correct
- B. destroy
- C. end
- D. list

20. RELEVANT   20.____
- A. conclusive
- B. careful
- C. obvious
- D. related

21. VERIFY   21.____
- A. challenge
- B. change
- C. confirm
- D. reveal

22. INSIGNIFICANT   22.____
- A. incorrect
- B. limited
- C. unimportant
- D. undesirable

23. RESCIND   23.____
- A. annul
- B. deride
- C. extol
- D. indulge

24. AUGMENT   24.____
- A. alter
- B. increase
- C. obey
- D. perceive

25. AUTONOMOUS   25.____
- A. conceptual
- B. constant
- C. defamatory
- D. independent

26. TRANSCRIPT   26.____
- A. copy
- B. report
- C. sentence
- D. termination

27. DISCORDANT   27.____
- A. quarrelsome
- B. comprised
- C. effusive
- D. harmonious

28. DISTEND   28.____
- A. constrict
- B. dilate
- C. redeem
- D. silence

29. EMANATE

    A. bridge   B. coherency   C. conquer   D. flow

29.___

30. EXULTANT

    A. easily upset   B. in high spirits
    C. subject to moods   D. very much over-priced

30.___

_____

KEY (CORRECT ANSWERS)

1.	B	11.	D	21.	C
2.	B	12.	A	22.	C
3.	A	13.	A	23.	A
4.	C	14.	B	24.	B
5.	C	15.	A	25.	D
6.	D	16.	B	26.	A
7.	C	17.	B	27.	A
8.	C	18.	A	28.	B
9.	A	19.	A	29.	D
10.	C	20.	D	30.	B

_____

SPELLING
EXAMINATION SECTION
TEST 1

DIRECTIONS: Each question or incomplete statement is followed by several suggested answers or completions. Select the one that BEST answers the question or completes the statement. *PRINT THE LETTER OF THE CORRECT ANSWER IN THE SPACE AT THE RIGHT.*

Questions 1-5.

DIRECTIONS: Questions 1 through 5 consist of four words. Indicate the letter of the word that is CORRECTLY spelled.

1. A. harassment   B. harrasment   1.____
    C. harasment   D. harrassment

2. A. maintainance   B. maintenence   2.____
    C. maintainence   D. maintenance

3. A. comparable   B. comprable   3.____
    C. comparible   D. commparable

4. A. suficient   B. suffciant   4.____
    C. sufficient   D. suficiant

5. A. fairly   B. fairley   C. farely   D. fairlie   5.____

Questions 6-10.

DIRECTIONS: Questions 6 through 10 consist of four words. Indicate the letter of the word that is INCORRECTLY spelled.

6. A. pallor   B. ballid   C. ballet   D. pallid   6.____

7. A. urbane   B. surburbane
    C. interurban   D. urban

8. A. facial   B. physical   C. fiscle   D. muscle   8.____

9. A. interceed   B. benefited
    C. analogous   D. altogether

10. A. seizure   B. irrelevant
    C. inordinate   D. dissapproved

KEY (CORRECT ANSWERS)

1.	A	6.	B
2.	D	7.	B
3.	A	8.	C
4.	C	9.	A
5.	A	10.	D

TEST 2

DIRECTIONS: Each of Questions 1 through 15 consists of two words preceded by the letters A and B. In each question, one of the words may be spelled INCORRECTLY or both words may be spelled CORRECTLY. If one of the words in a question is spelled INCORRECTLY, print in the space at the right the capital letter preceding the INCORRECTLY spelled word. If both words are spelled CORRECTLY, print the letter C.

1.	A. easely	B. readily	1._____
2.	A. pursue	B. decend	2._____
3.	A. measure	B. laboratory	3._____
4.	A. exausted	B. traffic	4._____
5.	A. discussion	B. unpleasant	5._____
6.	A. campaign	B. murmer	6._____
7.	A. guarantee	B. sanatary	7._____
8.	A. communication	B. safty	8._____
9.	A. numerus	B. celebration	9._____
10.	A. nourish	B. begining	10._____
11.	A. courious	B. witness	11._____
12.	A. undoubtedly	B. thoroughly	12._____
13.	A. accessible	B. artifical	13._____
14.	A. feild	B. arranged	14._____
15.	A. admittence	B. hastily	15._____

KEY (CORRECT ANSWERS)

1.	A	6.	B	11.	A
2.	B	7.	B	12.	C
3.	C	8.	B	13.	B
4.	A	9.	A	14.	A
5.	C	10.	B	15.	A

TEST 3

DIRECTIONS: In each of the following sentences, one word is misspelled. Following each sentence is a list of four words taken from the sentence. Indicate the letter of the word which is MISSPELLED in the sentence. *PRINT THE LETTER OF THE CORRECT ANSWER IN THE SPACE AT THE RIGHT.*

1. The placing of any inflammable substance in any building, or the placing of any device or contrivence capable of producing fire, for the purpose of causing a fire is an attempt to burn.

    A. inflammable   B. substance
    C. device   D. contrivence

1.____

2. The word *break* also means obtaining an entrance into a building by any artifice used for that purpose, or by colussion with any person therein.

    A. obtaining   B. entrance
    C. artifice   D. colussion

2.____

3. Any person who with intent to provoke a breech of the peace causes a disturbance or is offensive to others may be deemed to have committed disorderly conduct.

    A. breech   B. disturbance
    C. offensive   D. committed

3.____

4. When the offender inflicts a grevious harm upon the person from whose possession, or in whose presence, property is taken, he is guilty of robbery.

    A. offender   B. grevious
    C. possession   D. presence

4.____

5. A person who willfully encourages or advises another person in attempting to take the latter's life is guilty of a felony.

    A. willfully   B. encourages
    C. advises   D. attempting

5.____

6. He maliciously demurred to an ajournment of the proceedings.

    A. maliciously   B. demurred
    C. ajournment   D. proceedings

6.____

7. His innocence at that time is irrelevant in view of his more recent villianous demeanor.

    A. innocence   B. irrelevant
    C. villianous   D. demeanor

7.____

8. The mischievous boys aggrevated the annoyance of their neighbor.

    A. mischievous   B. aggrevated
    C. annoyance   D. neighbor

8.____

9. While his perseverence was commendable, his judgment was debatable.

    A. perseverence   B. commendable
    C. judgment   D. debatable

9.____

10. He was hoping the appeal would facilitate his aquittal.   10._____

    A. hoping   B. appeal
    C. facilitate   D. aquittal

11. It would be preferable for them to persue separate courses.   11._____

    A. preferable   B. persue
    C. separate   D. courses

12. The litigant was complimented on his persistance and achievement.   12._____

    A. litigant   B. complimented
    C. persistance   D. achievement

13. Ocassionally there are discrepancies in the descriptions of miscellaneous items.   13._____

    A. ocassionally   B. discrepancies
    C. descriptions   D. miscellaneous

14. The councilmanic seargent-at-arms enforced the prohibition.   14._____

    A. councilmanic   B. seargent-at-arms
    C. enforced   D. prohibition

15. The teacher had an ingenious device for maintaning attendance.   15._____

    A. ingenious   B. device
    C. maintaning   D. attendance

16. A worrysome situation has developed as a result of the assessment that absenteeism is   16._____
increasing despite our conscientious efforts.

    A. worrysome   B. assessment
    C. absenteeism   D. conscientious

17. I concurred with the credit manager that it was practicable to charge purchases on a   17._____
biennial basis, and the company agreed to adhear to this policy.

    A. concurred   B. practicable
    C. biennial   D. adhear

18. The pastor was chagrined and embarassed by the irreverent conduct of one of his   18._____
parishioners.

    A. chagrined   B. embarassed
    C. irreverent   D. parishioners

19. His inate seriousness was belied by his flippant demeanor.   19._____

    A. inate   B. belied
    C. flippant   D. demeanor

20. It was exceedingly regrettable that the excessive number   20._____
of challanges in the court delayed the start of the trial.

    A. exceedingly   B. regrettable
    C. excessive   D. challanges

KEY (CORRECT ANSWERS)

1.	D	11.	B
2.	D	12.	C
3.	A	13.	A
4.	B	14.	B
5.	A	15.	C
6.	C	16.	A
7.	C	17.	D
8.	B	18.	B
9.	A	19.	A
10.	D	20.	D

———

TEST 4

Questions 1-11.

DIRECTIONS: Each question consists of three words. In each question, one of the words may be spelled incorrectly or all three may be spelled correctly. For each question, if one of the words is spelled INCORRECTLY, write the letter of the incorrect word in the space at the right. If all three words are spelled CORRECTLY, write the letter D in the space at the right.

SAMPLE I: (A) guide (B) department (C) stranger
SAMPLE II: (A) comply (B) valuable (C) window
In Sample I, departmint is incorrect. It should be spelled department. Therefore, B is the answer.
In Sample II, all three words are spelled correctly. Therefore, D is the answer.

1.	A.	argument	B.	reciept	C.	complain	1._____
2.	A.	sufficient	B.	postpone	C.	visible	2._____
3.	A.	expirience	B.	dissatisfy	C.	alternate	3._____
4.	A.	occurred	B.	noticable	C.	appendix	4._____
5.	A.	anxious	B.	guarantee	C.	calender	5._____
6.	A.	sincerely	B.	affectionately	C.	truly	6._____
7.	A.	excellant	B.	verify	C.	important	7._____
8.	A.	error	B.	quality	C.	enviroment	8._____
9.	A.	exercise	B.	advance	C.	pressure	9._____
10.	A.	citizen	B.	expence	C.	memory	10._____
11.	A.	flexable	B.	focus	C.	forward	11._____

Questions 12-15.

DIRECTIONS: Each of Questions 12 through 15 consists of a group of four words. Examine each group carefully; then in the space at the right, indicate
A - if only one word in the group is spelled correctly
B - if two words in the group are spelled correctly
C - if three words in the group are spelled correctly
D - if all four words in the group are spelled correctly

12.   Wendsday, particular, similar, hunderd   12._____

13.   realize, judgment, opportunities, consistent   13._____

14.   equel, principle, assistense, commitee   14._____

15.   simultaneous, privilege, advise, ocassional   15._____

KEY (CORRECT ANSWERS)

1.	B	6.	D	11.	A
2.	D	7.	A	12.	B
3.	A	8.	C	13.	D
4.	B	9.	D	14.	A
5.	C	10.	B	15.	C

———

TEST 5

DIRECTIONS: Each of Questions 1 through 15 consists of two words preceded by the letters A and B. In each item, one of the words may be spelled INCORRECTLY or both words may be spelled CORRECTLY. If one of the words in a question is spelled INCORRECTLY, print in the space at the right the letter preceding the INCORRECTLY spelled word. If both words are spelled CORRECTLY, print the letter C.

1.	A.	justified	B.	offering	1.
2.	A.	predjudice	B.	license	2.
3.	A.	label	B.	pamphlet	3.
4.	A.	bulletin	B.	physical	4.
5.	A.	assure	B.	exceed	5.
6.	A.	advantagous	B.	evident	6.
7.	A.	benefit	B.	occured	7.
8.	A.	acquire	B.	graditude	8.
9.	A.	amenable	B.	boundry	9.
10.	A.	deceive	B.	voluntary	10.
11.	A.	imunity	B.	conciliate	11.
12.	A.	acknoledge	B.	presume	12.
13.	A.	substitute	B.	prespiration	13.
14.	A.	reputable	B.	announce	14.
15.	A.	luncheon	B.	wretched	15.

KEY (CORRECT ANSWERS)

1.	C	6.	A	11.	A
2.	A	7.	B	12.	A
3.	C	8.	B	13.	B
4.	C	9.	B	14.	A
5.	C	10.	C	15.	C

TEST 6

DIRECTIONS: Questions 1 through 15 contain lists of words, one of which is misspelled. Indicate the MISSPELLED word in each group. *PRINT THE LETTER OF THE CORRECT ANSWER IN THE SPACE AT THE RIGHT.*

1.   A. felony   B. lacerate
       C. cancellation   D. seperate

2.   A. batallion   B. beneficial
       C. miscellaneous   D. secretary

3.   A. camouflage   B. changeable   C. embarass   D. inoculate   3._____

4.   A. beneficial   B. disasterous
       C. incredible   D. miniature

5.   A. auxilliary   B. hypocrisy   C. phlegm   D. vengeance   5._____

6.   A. aisle   B. cemetary
       C. courtesy   D. extraordinary

7.   A. crystallize   B. innoculate
       C. eminent   D. symmetrical

8.   A. judgment   B. maintainance
       C. bouillon   D. eery

9.   A. isosceles   B. ukulele   C. mayonaise   D. iridescent   9._____

10.   A. remembrance   B. occurence
        C. correspondence   D. countenance

11.   A. corpuscles   B. mischievous
        C. batchelor   D. bulletin

12.   A. terrace   B. banister   C. concrete   D. masonery   12._____

13.   A. balluster   B. gutter   C. latch   D. bridging   13._____

14.   A. personnell   B. navel   C. therefor   D. emigrant   14._____

15.   A. committee   B. submiting   15._____
        C. amendment   D. electorate

KEY (CORRECT ANSWERS)

1.	D	6.	B	11.	C
2.	A	7.	B	12.	D
3.	C	8.	B	13.	A
4.	B	9.	C	14.	A
5.	A	10.	B	15.	B

TEST 7

Questions 1-5.

DIRECTIONS:　Questions 1 through 5 consist of groups of four words. Select answer:
　　　　　A if only ONE word is spelled correctly in a group
　　　　　B if TWO words are spelled correctly in a group
　　　　　C if THREE words are spelled correctly in a group
　　　　　D if all FOUR words are spelled correctly in a group

1.　counterfeit,　embarass,　panicky,　supercede　　　　　　1.____

2.　counterfeit,　embarass,　panicky,　supercede　　　　　　2.____

3.　bankruptcy　describable,　proceed,　vacuum　　　　　　3.____

4.　handicapped,　mispell,　offerred,　pilgrimmage　　　　　4.____

5.　corduroy,　interfere,　privilege,　eparator　　　　　　5.____

Questions 6-10.

DIRECTIONS:　Questions 6 through 10 consist of four pairs of words each. Some of the words
　　　　　are spelled correctly; others are spelled incorrectly. For each question, indi-
　　　　　cate in the space at the right the letter preceding that pair of words in which
　　　　　BOTH words are spelled CORRECTLY.

6.　A.　hygienic, inviegle　　　　　B.　omniscience, pittance　　6.____
　　C.　plagarize, nullify　　　　　D.　seargent, perilous

7.　A.　auxilary, existence　　　　　B.　pronounciation, accordance　7.____
　　C.　ignominy, indegence　　　　　D.　suable, baccalaureate

8.　A.　discreet, inaudible　　　　　B.　hypocrisy, currupt　　8.____
　　C.　liquidate, maintainance　　　D.　transparancy, onerous

9.　A.　facility, stimulent　　　　　B.　frugel, sanitary　　9.____
　　C.　monetary, prefatory　　　　　D.　punctileous, credentials

10.　A.　bankruptsy, perceptible　　　B.　disuade, resilient　　10.____
　　　C.　exhilerate, expectancy　　　D.　panegyric, disparate

Questions 11-15

DIRECTIONS:　Each question or incomplete statement is followed by several suggested
　　　　　answers or completions. Select the one that BEST answers the question or
　　　　　completes the statement. *PRINT THE LETTER OF THE CORRECT ANSWER
　　　　　IN THE SPACE AT THE RIGHT.*

11.　The silent *e* must be retained when the suffix *-able* is added to the word　　11.____

　　　A.　argue　　　　B.　love　　　　C.　move　　　　D.　notice

12.　The CORRECTLY spelled word in the choices below is　　12.____

　　　A.　kindergarden　　　　　　　B.　zylophone
　　　C.　hemorrhage　　　　　　　D.　mayonaise

13. Of the following words, the one spelled CORRECTLY is

    A. begger   B. cemetary
    C. embarassed   D. coyote

13.____

14. Of the following words, the one spelled CORRECTLY is

    A. dandilion   B. wiry   C. sieze   D. rythmic

14.____

15. Of the following words, the one spelled CORRECTLY is

    A. beligerent   B. anihilation
    C. facetious   D. adversery

15.____

KEY (CORRECT ANSWERS)

1.	B	6.	B	11.	D
2.	C	7.	D	12.	C
3.	D	8.	A	13.	D
4.	A	9.	C	14.	B
5.	D	10.	D	15.	C

TEST 8

DIRECTIONS: In each of the following sentences, one word is misspelled. Following each sentence is a list of four words taken from the sentence. Indicate the letter of the word which is MISSPELLED. *PRINT THE LETTER OF THE CORRECT ANSWER IN THE SPACE AT THE RIGHT.*

1. If the administrator attempts to withold information, there is a good likelihood that there will be serious repercussions.

   A. administrator
   C. likelihood
   B. withold
   D. repercussions

1.____

2. He condescended to apologize, but we felt that a beligerent person should not occupy an influential position.

   A. condescended
   C. beligerent
   B. apologize
   D. influential

2.____

3. Despite the sporadic delinquent payments of his indebtedness, Mr. Johnson has been an exemplery customer.

   A. sporadic
   C. indebtedness
   B. delinquent
   D. exemplery

3.____

4. He was appreciative of the support he consistantly acquired, but he felt that he had waited an inordinate length of time for it.

   A. appreciative
   C. acquired
   B. consistantly
   D. inordinate

4.____

5. Undeniably they benefited from the establishment of a receivership, but the question of statutary limitations remained unresolved.

   A. undeniably
   C. receivership
   B. benefited
   D. statutary

5.____

6. Mr. Smith profered his hand as an indication that he considered it a viable contract, but Mr. Nelson alluded to the fact that his colleagues had not been consulted.

   A. profered
   C. alluded
   B. viable
   D. colleagues

6.____

7. The treatments were beneficial according to the optometrists, and the consensus was that minimal improvement could be expected.

   A. beneficial
   C. consensus
   B. optomotrists
   D. minimal

7.____

8. Her frivalous manner was unbecoming because the air of solemnity at the cemetery was pervasive.

   A. frivalous
   C. cemetery
   B. solemnity
   D. pervasive

8.____

9. The clandestine meetings were designed to make the two adversaries more amicable, but they served only to intensify their emnity.

   A. clandestine
   C. amicable
   B. adversaries
   D. emnity

9.____

10. Do you think that his innovative ideas and financial acumen will help stabalize the fluctu-   10.____
    ations of the stock market?

    A. innovative   B. acumen
    C. stabalize   D. fluctuations

11. In order to keep a perpetual inventory, you will have to keep an uninterrupted surveil-   11.____
    lance of all the miscellanious stock.

    A. perpetual   B. uninterrupted
    C. surveillance   D. miscellanious

12. She used the art of pursuasion on the children because she found that caustic remarks   12.____
    had no perceptible effect on their behavior.

    A. pursuasion   B. caustic
    C. perceptible   D. effect

13. His sacreligious outbursts offended his constituents, and he was summarily removed   13.____
    from office by the City Council.

    A. sacreligious   B. constituents
    C. summarily   D. Council

14. They exhorted the contestants to greater efforts, but the exhorbitant costs in terms of   14.____
    energy expended resulted in a feeling of lethargy.

    A. exhorted   B. contestants
    C. exhorbitant   D. lethargy

15. Since he was knowledgable about illicit drugs, he was served with a subpoena to appear   15.____
    for the prosecution.

    A. knowledgable   B. illicit
    C. subpoena   D. prosecution

16. In spite of his lucid statements, they denigrated his report and decided it should be suc-   16.____
    cintly paraphrased.

    A. lucid   B. denigrated
    C. succintly   D. paraphrased

17. The discussion was not germane to the contraversy, but the indicted man's insistence on   17.____
    further talk was allowed.

    A. germane   B. contraversy
    C. indicted   D. insistence

18. The legislators were enervated by the distances they had traveled during the election   18.____
    year to fullfil their speaking engagements.

    A. legislators   B. enervated
    C. traveled   D. fullfil

19. The plaintiffs' attorneis charged the defendant in the case with felonious assault.   19.____

   A. plaintiffs'   B. attorneis
   C. defendant   D. felonious

20. It is symptomatic of the times that we try to placate all, but a proposal for new forms of   20.____
    disciplinery action was promulgated by the staff.

   A. symptomatic   B. placate
   C. disciplinery   D. promulgated

KEY (CORRECT ANSWERS)

1.	B	6.	A	11.	D	16.	C
2.	C	7.	B	12.	A	17.	B
3.	D	8.	A	13.	A	18.	D
4.	B	9.	D	14.	C	19.	B
5.	D	10.	C	15.	A	20.	C

TEST 9

DIRECTIONS: Each of Questions 1 through 15 consists of a single word which is spelled either correctly or incorrectly. If the word is spelled CORRECTLY, you are to print the letter C (Correct) in the space at the right. If the word is spelled INCORRECTLY, you are to print the letter W (Wrong).

1.   pospone   1.____

2.   diffrent   2.____

3.   height   3.____

4.   carefully   4.____

5.   ability   5.____

6.   temper   6.____

7.   deslike   7.____

8.   seldem   8.____

9.   alcohol   9.____

10.   expense   10.____

11.   vegatable   11.____

12.   dispensary   12.____

13.   specemin   13.____

14.   allowance   14.____

15.   exersise   15.____

―――――

KEY (CORRECT ANSWERS)

1.	W	6.	C	11.	W
2.	W	7.	W	12.	C
3.	C	8.	W	13.	W
4.	C	9.	C	14.	C
5.	C	10.	C	15.	W

―――――

TEST 10

DIRECTIONS: Each of Questions 1 through 10 consists of four words, one of which may be spelled incorrectly or all four words may be spelled correctly. If one of the words in a question is spelled incorrectly, print in the space at the right the capital letter preceding the word which is spelled INCORRECTLY. If all four words are spelled CORRECTLY, print the letter E.

1.	A.	dismissal	B.	collateral	C.	leisure	D.	proffession
2.	A.	subsidary	B.	outrageous	C.	liaison	D.	assessed
3.	A.	already	B.	changeable	C.	mischevous	D.	cylinder
4.	A.	supersede	B.	deceit	C.	dissension	D.	imminent
5.	A.	arguing	B.	contagious	C.	comparitive	D.	accessible
6.	A.	indelible	B.	existance	C.	presumptuous	D.	mileage
7.	A.	extention	B.	aggregate	C.	sustenance	D.	gratuitous
8.	A.	interrogate	B.	exaggeration	C.	vacillate	D.	moreover
9.	A.	parallel	B.	derogatory	C.	admissable	D.	appellate
10.	A.	safety	B.	cumalative	C.	disappear	D.	usable

1. ___
2. ___
3. ___
4. ___
5. ___
6. ___
7. ___
8. ___
9. ___
10. ___

KEY (CORRECT ANSWERS)

1.	D		6.	B
2.	A		7.	A
3.	C		8.	E
4.	E		9.	C
5.	C		10.	B

TEST 11

DIRECTIONS: Each of Questions 1 through 10 consists of four words, one of which may be spelled incorrectly or all four words may be spelled correctly. If one of the words in a question is spelled INCORRECTLY, print in the space at the right the capital letter preceding the word which is spelled incorrectly. If all four words are spelled CORRECTLY, print the letter E.

1.	A. vehicular		B. gesticulate		1.____
	C. manageable		D. fullfil		
2.	A. inovation		B. onerous		2.____
	C. chastise		D. irresistible		
3.	A. familiarize		B. dissolution		3.____
	C. oscillate		D. superflous		
4.	A. census		B. defender		4.____
	C. adherence		D. inconceivable		
5.	A. voluminous		B. liberalize		5.____
	C. bankrupcy		D. conversion		
6.	A. justifiable		B. executor		6.____
	C. perpatrate		D. dispelled		
7.	A. boycott		B. abeyence		7.____
	C. enterprise		D. circular		
8.	A. spontaineous		B. dubious		8.____
	C. analyze		D. premonition		
9.	A. intelligible		B. apparently		9.____
	C. genuine		D. crucial		
10.	A. plentiful		B. ascertain		10.____
	C. carreer		D. preliminary		

KEY (CORRECT ANSWERS)

1.	D		6.	C
2.	A		7.	B
3.	D		8.	A
4.	E		9.	E
5.	C		10.	C

TEST 12

DIRECTIONS: Questions 1 through 25 consist of four words each, of which one of the words may be spelled incorrectly or all four words may be spelled correctly. If one of the words in a question is spelled INCORRECTLY, print in the space at the right the capital letter preceding the word which is spelled incorrectly. If all four words are spelled CORRECTLY, print the letter E.

1. A. temporary   B. existance   1. ____
    C. complimentary D. altogether

2. A. privilege   B. changeable   2. ____
    C. jeopardize   D. commitment

3. A. grievous   B. alloted   3. ____
    C. outrageous   D. mortgage

4. A. tempermental   B. accommodating   4. ____
    C. bookkeeping   D. panicky

5. A. auxiliary   B. indispensable   5. ____
    C. ecstasy   D. fiery

6. A. dissappear   B. buoyant   6. ____
    C. imminent   D. parallel

7. A. loosly   B. medicine   7. ____
    C. schedule   D. defendant

8. A. endeavor   B. persuade   8. ____
    C. retroactive   D. desparate

9. A. usage   B. servicable   9. ____
    C. disadvantageous D. remittance

10. A. beneficary   B. receipt   10. ____
    C. excitable   D. implement

11. A. accompanying   B. intangible   11. ____
    C. offerred   D. movable

12. A. controlling   B. seize   12. ____
    C. repetitious   D. miscellaneous

13. A. installation   B. accommodation   13. ____
    C. consistant   D. illuminate

14. A. incidentaly   B. privilege   14. ____
    C. apparent   D. chargeable

15. A. prevalent   B. serial   15. ____
    C. briefly   D. disatisfied

16. A. reciprocal   B. concurrence   16.____
     C. persistence   D. withold

17. A. deferred   B. suing   17.____
     C. fulfilled   D. pursuant

18. A. questionnable   B. omission   18.____
     C. acknowledgment   D. insistent

19. A. guarantee   B. committment   19.____
     C. mitigate   D. publicly

20. A. prerogative   B. apprise   20.____
     C. extrordinary   D. continual

21. A. arrogant   B. handicapped   21.____
     C. judicious   D. perennial

22. A. permissable   B. deceive   22.____
     C. innumerable   D. retrieve

23. A. notable   B. allegiance   23.____
     C. reimburse   D. illegal

24. A. wholly   B. disbursement   24.____
     C. hindrance   D. conciliatory

25. A. guidance   B. condemn   25.____
     C. publically   D. coercion

KEY (CORRECT ANSWERS)

1.	B		11.	C
2.	E		12.	E
3.	B		13.	C
4.	A		14.	A
5.	E		15.	D
6.	A		16.	D
7.	A		17.	E
8.	D		18.	A
9.	B		19.	B
10.	A		20.	C

21.	E
22.	A
23.	E
24.	E
25.	C

CLERICAL ABILITIES

EXAMINATION SECTION
TEST 1

DIRECTIONS: Each question or incomplete statement is followed by several suggested answers or completions. Select the one that BEST answers the question or completes the statement. *PRINT THE LETTER OF THE CORRECT ANSWER IN THE SPACE AT THE RIGHT.*

Questions 1 through 4 are to be answered on the basis of the information below:

The most commonly used filing system and the one that is easiest to learn is alphabetical filing. This involves putting records in an A to Z order, according to the letters of the alphabet. The name of a person is filed by using the following order: first, the surname or last name; second, the first name; third, the middle name or initial. For example, *Henry C. Young* is filed under Yand thereafter under *Young, Henry C.* The name of a company is filed in the same way. For example, *Long Cabinet Co.* is filed under *L*, while *John T. Long Cabinet Co.* is filed under *L* and thereafter under *Long, John T. Cabinet Co.*

1. The one of the following which lists the names of the persons in the CORRECT alphabetical order is

    A.   Mary Carrie, Helen Carrol, James Carson, John Carter
    B.   James Carson, Mary Carrie, John Carter, Helen Carrol
    C.   Helen Carrol, James Carson, John Carter, Mary Carrie
    D.   John Carter, Helen Carrol, Mary Carrie, James Carson

1.____

2. The one of the following which lists the names of the persons in the CORRECT alphabetical order is

    A.   Jones, John C.; Jones, John A.; Jones, John P.; Jones, John K.
    B.   Jones, John P.; Jones, John K.; Jones, John C.; Jones, John A.
    C.   Jones, John A.; Jones, John C.; Jones, John K.; Jones, John P.
    D.   Jones, John K.; Jones, John C,; Jones, John A.; Jones, John P.

2.____

3. The one of the following which lists the names of the companies in CORRECT alphabetical order is

    A.   Blane Co., Blake Co., Block Co., Blear Co.
    B.   Blake Co., Blane Co., Blear Co., Block Co.
    C.   Block Co., Blear Co., Blane Co., Blake Co.
    D.   Blear Co., Blake Co., Blane Co., Block Co.

3.____

4. You are to return to the file an index card on *Barry C. Wayne Materials and Supplies Co.* Of the following, the CORRECT alphabetical group that you should return the index card to is

    A.   A to G   B.   H to M   C.   N to S   D.   T to Z

4.____

Questions 5-10

DIRECTIONS: In each of questions 5 through 10, the names of four people are given. For each question, choose as your answer the one of the four names given which would be filed FIRST according to the usual system of alphabetical filing of names, as described in the following paragraph.

In filing names, you must start with the last name. Names are filed in order of the first letter of the last name, then the second letter, etc. Therefore, BAILY would be filed by BROWN, which would be filed before COLT. A name with fewer letters of the same type comes first; i.e., Smith before Smithe. If the last names are the same, the names are filed alphabetically by the first name. If the first name is an initial, a name with an initial would come before a first name that starts with the same letter as the initial. Therefore, I. BROWN would come before IRA BROWN. Finally, if both last name and first name are the same, the name would be filed alphabetically by the middle name, once again an initial coming before a middle name which starts with the same letter as the initial. If there is no middle name at all, the name would come before those with middle initials or names.

Sample Question:

A.	Lester Daniels
B.	William Dancer
C.	Nathan Danzig
D.	Dan Lester

The last names beginning with D are filed before the last name beginning with L. Since DANIELS, DANCER and DANZIG all begin with the same three letters, you must look at the fourth letter of the last name to determine which name should be filed first. C comes before I or Z, so DANCER is filed before DANIELS or DANZIG. Therefore, the answer to the question is B.

5.   A. Scott Biala   B. Mary Byala   5._____
     C. Martin Baylor   D. Francis Bauer

6.   A. Howard J. Black   B. Howard Black
     C. J. Howard Black   D. John H. Black

7.   A. Theodora Garth Kingston   B. Theadore Barth Kingston   7._____
     C. Paulette Mary Huerta   D. Paul M. Huerta

8.   A. Paulette Mary Huerta   B. Paul M. Huerta   8._____
     C. Paulette L. Huerta   D. Peter A. Huerta

9.   A. Martha Hunt Morgan   B. Martin Hunt Morgan   9._____
     C. Mary H. Morgan   D. Martine H. Morgan

10. A. James T. Meerschaum   B. James M. Mershum   10._____
     C. James F. Mearshaum   D. James N. Meshum

Questions 11 through 14 are to be answered on the basis of the following information:

You are required to file various documents in file drawers which are labeled according to the following pattern:

DOCUMENTS

MEMOS			LETTERS	
File	Subject		File	Subject
84PM1	(A-L)		84PC1	(A-L)
84PM2	(M-Z)		84PC2	(M-Z)
REPORTS			INQUIRIES	
File	Subject		File	Subject
84PR1	(A-L)		84PQ1	(A-L)
84PR2	(M-Z)		84PQ2	(M-Z)

11. A letter dealing with a burglary should be filed in the drawer labeled   11._____

    A. 84PM1   B. 84PC1   C. 84PR1   D. 84PQ2

12. A report on Statistics should be found in the drawer labeled   12._____

    A. 84PM1   B. 84PC2   C. 84PR2   D. 84PQ2

13. An inquiry is received about parade permit procedures. It should be filed in the drawer   13._____
    labeled

    A. 84PM2   B. 84PC1   C. 84PR1   D. 84PQ2

14. A police officer has a question about a robbery report you filed. You should pull this file   14._____
    from the drawer labeled

    A. 84PM1   B. 84PM2   C. 84PR1   D. 84PR2

Questions 15-22

DIRECTIONS: Each of questions 15 through 22 consist of four or six numbered names. For
              each question, choose the option which indicates the order in which the
              names should be filed in accordance with the following filing instructions:
    • File alphabetically according to last name, then first name, then middle initial
    • File according to each successive letter within a name
    • When comparing two names in which the letters in the longer name are identical to
      the corresponding letters in the shorter name, the shorter name is filed first
    • When the last names are the same, initials are always filed before names beginning
      with the same letter

15.   I.   Ralph Robinson   II.   Alfred Ross   15._____
      III.   Luis Robles   IV.   James Roberts

    The CORRECT filing sequence for the above names should be
    A. IV, II, I, III   B. I, IV, III, II
    C. III, IV, I, II   D. IV, I, III, II

16.
   I.   Irwin Goodwin
  III. Irene Goodman
   V. Ruth I. Goldstein
   II. Inez Gonzalez
  IV. Ira S.Goodwin
  VI. M.B. Goodman

The CORRECT filing sequence for the above names should be
  A. V, II, I, IV, III, VI
  B. V, II, VI, III, IV, I
  C. V, II, III, VI, IV, I
  D. V, II, III, VI, I, IV

17.
   I. George Allan
  III. Gary Allen
   II. Gregory Allen
  IV. George Allen

The CORRECT filing sequence for the above names should be
  A. IV, III, I, II
  B. I, IV, II, III
  C. III, IV, I, II
  D. I, III, IV, II

18.
   I. Simon Kauffman
  III. Robert Kaufmann
   II. Leo Kaufman
  IV. Paul Kauffman

The CORRECT filing sequence for the above names should be
  A. I, IV, II, III
  B. II, IV, III, I
  C. III, II, IV, I
  D. I, II, III, IV

19.
   I. Roberta Williams
  III. Roberta Wilson
   II. Robin Wilson
  IV. Robin Williams

The CORRECT filing sequence for the above names should be
  A. III, II, IV, I
  B. I, IV, III, II
  C. I, II, III, IV
  D. III, I, II, IV

20.
   I. Lawrence Shultz
  III. Theodore Schwartz
   V. Alvin Schultz
   II. Albert Schultz
  IV. Thomas Schwarz
  VI. Leonard Shultz

The CORRECT filing sequence for the above names should be
  A. II, V, III, IV, I, VI
  B. IV, III, V, I, II, VI
  C. II, V, I, VI, III, IV
  D. I, VI, II, V, III, IV

21.
   I. McArdle
  III. Maletz
   V. Meyer
   II. Mayer
  IV. McNiff
  VI. MacMahon

The CORRECT filing sequence for the above names should be
  A. I, IV, VI, III, II, V
  B. II, I, IV, VI, III, V
  C. VI, III, II, I, IV, V
  D. VI, III, II, V, I, IV

22.
   I. Jack E. Johnson
  III. Bertha Jackson
   V. Ann Johns
   II. R.H. Jackson
  IV. J.T. Johnson
  VI. John Jacobs

The CORRECT filing sequence for the above names should be
  A. II, III, VI, V, IV, I
  B. III, II, VI, V, IV, I
  C. VI, II, III, I, V, IV
  D. III, II, VI, IV, V, I

Questions 23-30

DIRECTIONS: The code table below shows 10 letters with matching numbers. For each question, there are three sets of letters. Each set of letters is followed by a set of numbers which may or may not match their correct letter according to the code table. For each question, check all three sets of letters and numbers and mark your answer:

A.   if no pairs are correctly matched
B.   if only one pair is correctly matched
C.   if only two pairs are correctly matched
D.   if all three pairs are correctly matched

CODE TABLE

T	M	V	D	S	P	R	G	B	H
1	2	3	4	5	6	7	8	9	0

Sample Question: TMVDSP - 123456
RGBHTM - 789011
DSPRGB - 256789

In the sample question above, the first set of numbers correctly matches its set of letters. But the second and third pairs contain mistakes. In the second pair, M is incorrectly matched with number 1. According to the code table, letter M should be correctly matched with number 2. In the third pair, the letter D is incorrectly matched with number 2. According to the code table, letter D should be correctly matched with number 4. Since only one of the pairs is correctly matched, the answer is B.

23.   RSBMRM   759262   23._____
GDSRVH   845730
VDBRTM   349713

24.   TGVSDR   183247   24._____
SMHRDP   520647
TRMHSR   172057

25.   DSPRGM   456782   25._____
MVDBHT   234902
HPMDBT   062491

26.   BVPTRD   936184   26._____
GDPHMB   807029
GMRHMV   827032

27. MGVRSH   283750
     TRDMBS   174295
     SPRMGV   567283   27.____

28. SGBSDM   489542
     MGHPTM   290612
     MPBMHT   269301   28.____

29. TDPBHM   146902
     VPBMRS   369275
     GDMBHM   842902   29.____

30. MVPTBV   236194
     PDRTMB   647128
     BGTMSM   981232   30.____

KEY (CORRECT ANSWERS)

1.	A	11.	B	21.	C
2.	C	12.	C	22.	B
3.	B	13.	D	23.	B
4.	D	14.	D	24.	B
5.	D	15.	D	25.	C
6.	B	16.	C	26.	A
7.	B	17.	D	27.	D
8.	B	18.	A	28.	A
9.	A	19.	B	29.	D
10.	C	20.	A	30.	A

TEST 2

DIRECTIONS: Each question or incomplete statement is followed by several suggested answers or completions. Select the one that BEST answers the question or completes the statement. *PRINT THE LETTER OF THE CORRECT ANSWER IN THE SPACE AT THE RIGHT.*

Questions 1-10

DIRECTIONS: Questions 1 through 10 each consist of two columns, each containing four lines of names, numbers and/or addresses. For each question, compare the lines in Column I with the lines in Column II to see if they match exactly, and mark your answer according to the following instructions:
- A. all four lines match exactly
- B. only three lines match exactly
- C. only two lines match exactly
- D. only one line matches exactly

Column I	Column II	
1. Earl Hodgson 1409870 Shore Ave. Macon Rd	Earl Hodgson 1408970 Schore Ave. Macon Rd.	1._____
2. 9671485 470 Astor Court Halprin, Phillip Frank D. Poliseo	9671485 470 Astor Court Halperin, Phillip Frank D. Poliseo	2._____
3. Tandem Associates 144-17 Northern Blvd. Alberta Forchi Kings Park, NY 10751	Tandom Associates 144-17 Northern Blvd. Albert Forchi Kings Point, NY 10751	3._____
4. Bertha C. McCormack Clayton, MO 976-4242 New City, NY 10951	Bertha C. McCormack Clayton, MO 976-4242 New City, NY 10951	4._____
5. George C. Morill Columbia, SC 29201 Louis Ingham 3406 Forest Ave.	George C. Morrill Columbia, SD 29201 Louis Ingham 3406 Forest Ave.	5._____
6. 506 S. Elliott Pl. Herbert Hall 4712 Rockaway Pkway 169E. 7 St.	506 S. Elliott Pl. Hurbert Hall 4712 Rockaway Pkway 169E. 7 St.	6._____

7. 345 Park Ave.   345 Park Pl.   7.____
   Colman Oven Corp.   Coleman Oven Corp.
   Robert Conte   Robert Conti
   6179846   6179846

8. Grigori Schierber   Grigori Schierber   8.____
   Des Moines, Iowa   Des Moines, Iowa
   Gouverneur Hospital   Gouverneur Hospital
   91-35CresskillPl.   91-35Cresskill Pl.

9. Jeffery Janssen   Jeffrey Janssen   9.____
   8041071   8041071
   40 Rockefeller Plaza   40 Rockefeller Plaza
   407 6 St.   406 7 St.

10. 5971996   5871996   10.____
    3113 Knickerbocker Ave.   3113 Knickerbocker Ave.
    8434 Boston Post Rd.   8424 Boston Post Rd.
    Penn Station   Penn Station

Questions 11-14

DIRECTIONS: Questions 11 through 14 are to be answered by looking at the four groups of
names and addresses listed below and then finding out the number of groups
that have their corresponding numbered lines exactly the same.

GROUP I   GROUP II
Line 1: Richmond General Hospital   Richman General Hospital
Line 2: Geriatric Clinic   Geriatric Clinic
Line 3: 3975 Paerdegat St.   3975 Peardegat St.
Line 4: Loudonville, New York 11538   Londonville, New York 11538
GROUP III   GROUP IV
Line 1: Richmond General Hospital   Richmend General Hospital
Line 2: Geriatric Clinic   Geriatric Clinic
Line 3: 3795 Paerdegat St.   3975 Paerdegat St.
Line 4: Loudonville, New York 11358   Loudonville, New York 11538

11. In how many groups is line 1 exactly the same?   11.____

   A. 2   B. 3   C. 4   D. None

12. In how many groups is line 2 exactly the same?   12.____

   A. 2   B. 3   C. 4   D. None

13. In how many groups is line 3 exactly the same?   13.____

   A. 2   B. 3   C. 4   D. None

14. In how many groups is line 4 exactly the same?   14.____

   A. 2   B. 3   C. 4   D. None

Questions 15-18

DIRECTIONS: Each of questions 15 through 18 has two lists of names and addresses. Each list contains three sets of names and addresses. Check each of the three sets in the list on the right to see if they are the same as the corresponding set in the list on the left. Mark your answers as follows:

    A. if none of the sets are the same
    B. if only one of the sets is the same
    C. if only two of the sets are the same
    D. if all three of the sets are the same

15. Mary T. Berlinger
2351 Hampton St.
Monsey, NY 20117

    Eduardo Benes
473 Kingston Avenue
Central Islip, NY 11734

    Alan Carrington Fuchs
17 Gnarled Hollow Road
Los Angeles, CA 91635

Mary T. Berlinger
2351 Hampton St.
Monsey, NY 20117

Eduardo Benes
473 Kingston Avenue
Central Islip, NY 11734

Alan Carrington Fuchs
17 Gnarled Hollow Road
Los Angeles, CA 91685

15._____

16. David John Jacobson
178 35 St. Apt. 4C
New York, NY 00927

    Ann-Marie Calonella
7243 South Ridge Blvd.
Bakersfield, CA 96714

    Pauline M. Thompson
872 Linden Ave.
Houston, Texas 70321

David John Jacobson
178 53 St. Apt. 4C
New York, NY 00927

Ann-Marie Calonella
7243 South Ridge Blvd.
Bakersfield, CA 96714

Pauline M. Thomson
872 Linden Ave.
Houston, Texas 70321

16._____

17. Chester LeRoy Masterton
152 Lacy Rd.
Kankakee, Ill. 54532

    William Maloney
S. LaCrosse Pla.
Wausau, Wisconsin 52146

    Cynthia V. Barnes
16 Pines Rd.
Greenpoint, Miss. 20376

Chester LeRoy Masterson
152 Lacy Rd.
Kankakee, Ill. 54532

William Maloney
S. LaCross Pla.
Wausau, Wisconsin 52146

Cynthia V. Barnes
16 Pines Rd.
Greenpoint, Miss. 20376

17._____

18.   Marcel Jean Frontenac   Marcel Jean Frontenac   18.____
      8 Burton On The Water   6 Burton On The Water
      Calender, Me. 01471   Calender, Me. 01471

      J. Scott Marsden   J. Scott Marsden
      174 S.Tipton St.   174 Tipton St.
      Cleveland, Ohio   Cleveland, Ohio

      Lawrence T. Haney   Lawrence T. Haney
      171 McDonough St.   171 McDonough St.
      Decatur, GA 31304   Decatur, GA 31304

Questions 19-26

DIRECTIONS: Each of questions 19 through 26 has two lists of numbers. Each list contains three sets of numbers. Check each of the three sets in the list on the right to see if they are the same as the corresponding set in the list on the left. Mark your answers as follows:

          A.   if none of the sets are the same
          B.   if only one of the sets is the same
          C.   if only two of the sets are the same
          D.   if all three of the sets are the same

19.   7354183476   7354983476   19.____
      4474747744   4474747774
      57914302311   57914902311

20.   7143592185   7143892185   20.____
      8344517699   8344518699
      9178531263   9178531263

21.   2572114731   257214731   21.____
      8806835476   8806835476
      8255831246   8255831246

22.   331476853821   331476858621   22.____
      6976658532996   6976655832996
      3766042113715   3766042113745

23.   8806663315   8806663315   23.____
      74477138449   74477138449
      211756663666   211756663666

24.   990006966996   99000696996   24.____
      53022219743   53022219843
      4171171117717   4171171177717

25.   24400222433004   24400222433004   25.____
      5300030055000355   5300030055500355
      20000075532002022   20000075532002022

26. 6111666406600001116   61116664066001116   26._____
     7111300117001100733   7111300117001100733
     26666446664476518   26666446664476518

Questions 27-30

DIRECTIONS: Questions 27 through 30 are to be answered by picking the answer which is in
             the correct numerical order, from the lowest to highest number, in each ques-
             tion.

27. A. 44533, 44518, 44516, 44547   27._____
     B. 44516, 44518, 44533, 44547
     C. 44547, 44533, 44518, 44516
     D. 44518, 44516, 44547, 44533

28. A. 95587, 95593, 95601, 95620   28._____
     B. 95601, 95620, 95587, 95593
     C. 95593, 95587, 95601, 95620
     D. 95620, 95601, 95593, 95587

29. A. 232212, 232208, 232232, 232223   29._____
     B. 232208, 232223, 232212, 232232
     C. 232208, 232212, 232223, 232232
     D. 232223, 232232, 232208, 232212

30. A. 113419, 113521, 113462, 113588   30._____
     B. 113588, 113462, 113521, 113419
     C. 113521, 113588, 113419, 113462
     D. 113419, 113462, 113521, 113588

KEY (CORRECT ANSWERS)

1.	C	11.	A	21.	C
2.	B	12.	C	22.	A
3.	D	13.	A	23.	D
4.	A	14.	A	24.	A
5.	C	15.	C	25.	C
6.	B	16.	B	26.	C
7.	D	17.	B	27.	B
8.	A	18.	B	28.	A
9.	D	19.	B	29.	C
10.	C	20.	B	30.	D

READING COMPREHENSION
UNDERSTANDING AND INTERPRETING WRITTEN MATERIAL

EXAMINATION SECTION
TEST 1

DIRECTIONS: Each question or incomplete statement is followed by several suggested answers or completions. Select the one that BEST answers the question or completes the statement. *PRINT THE LETTER OF THE CORRECT ANSWER IN THE SPACE AT THE RIGHT.*

Questions 1-5.

DIRECTIONS: Questions 1 through 5 are to be answered on the basis of the following passage.

The laws with which criminal courts are concerned contain threats of punishment for infraction of specified rules. Consequently, the courts are organized primarily for implementation of the punitive societal reaction of crime. While the informal organization of most courts allows the judge to use discretion as to which guilty persons actually are to be punished, the threat of punishment for all guilty persons always is present. Also, in recent years a number of formal provisions for the use of non-punitive and treatment methods by the criminal courts have been made, but the threat of punishment remains, even for the recipients of the treatment and non-punitive measures. For example, it has become possible for courts to grant probation, which can be non-punitive, to some offenders, but the probationer is constantly under the threat of punishment, for, if he does not maintain the conditions of his probation, he may be imprisoned. As the treatment reaction to crime becomes more popular, the criminal courts may have as their sole function the determination of the guilt or innocence of the accused persons, leaving the problem of correcting criminals entirely to outsiders. Under such conditions, the organization of the court system, the duties and activities of court personnel, and the nature of the trial all would be decidedly different.

1. Which one of the following is the BEST description of the subject matter of the above passage?
   The

   A. value of non-punitive measures for criminals
   B. effect of punishment on guilty individuals
   C. punitive functions of the criminal courts
   D. success of probation as a deterrent of crime

1.____

2. It may be INFERRED from the above passage that the present traditional organization of the criminal court system is a result of

   A. the nature of the laws with which these courts are concerned
   B. a shift from non-punitive to punitive measures for correctional purposes
   C. an informal arrangement between court personnel and the government
   D. a formal decision made by court personnel to increase efficiency

2.____

3. All persons guilty of breaking certain specified rules, according to the above passage, are subject to the threat of

    A. treatment   B. punishment
    C. probation   D. retrial

3.____

4. According to the above passage, the decision whether or not to punish a guilty person is a function USUALLY performed by

    A. the jury   B. the criminal code
    C. the judge   D. corrections personnel

4.____

5. According to the above passage, which one of the following is a possible effect of an increase in the *treatment reactions to crime?*

    A. A decrease in the number of court personnel
    B. An increase in the number of criminal trials
    C. Less reliance on probation as a non-punitive treatment measure
    D. A decrease in the functions of the court following determination of guilt

5.____

Questions 6-8.

DIRECTIONS: Questions 6 through 8 are to be answered on the basis of the following passage.

    A glaring exception to the usual practice of the judicial trial as a means of conflict resolution is the utilization of administrative hearings. The growing tendency to create administrative bodies with rule-making and quasi-judicial powers has shattered many standard concepts. A comprehensive examination of the legal process cannot neglect these newer patterns.

    In the administrative process, the legislative, executive, and judicial functions are mixed together, and many functions, such as investigating, advocating, negotiating, testifying, rule making, and adjudicating, are carried out by the same agency. The reason for the breakdown of the separation-of-powers formula is not hard to find. It was felt by Congress, and state and municipal legislatures, that certain regulatory tasks could not be performed efficiently, rapidly, expertly, and with due concern for the public interest by the traditional branches of government. Accordingly, regulatory agencies were delegated powers to consider disputes from the earliest stage of investigation to the final stages of adjudication entirely within each agency itself, subject only to limited review in the regular courts.

6. The above passage states that the usual means for conflict resolution is through the use of

    A. judicial trial   B. administrative hearing
    C. legislation   D. regulatory agencies

6.____

7. The above passage IMPLIES that the use of administrative hearing in resolving conflict is a(n) _____ approach.

    A. traditional   B. new
    C. dangerous   D. experimental

7.____

8. The above passage states that the reason for the breakdown of the separation-of-powers formula in the administrative process is that

8.____

A. Congress believed that certain regulatory tasks could be better performed by separate agencies
B. legislative and executive functions are incompatible in the same agency
C. investigative and regulatory functions are not normally reviewed by the courts
D. state and municipal legislatures are more concerned with efficiency than with legality

Questions 9-10.

DIRECTIONS: Questions 9 and 10 are to be answered SOLELY on the basis of the information given in the following paragraph.

An assumption commonly made in regard to the reliability of testimony is that when a number of persons report upon the same matter, those details upon which there is an agreement may, in general, be considered as substantiated. Experiments have shown, however, that there is a tendency for the same errors to appear in the testimony of different individuals, and that, quite apart from any collusion, agreement of testimony is no proof of dependability.

9. According to the above paragraph, it is commonly assumed that details of an event are substantiated when   9.____

A. a number of persons report upon them
B. a reliable person testifies to them
C. no errors are apparent in the testimony of different individuals
D. several witnesses are in agreement about them

10. According to the above paragraph, agreement in the testimony of different witnesses to the same event is   10.____

A. evaluated more reliably when considered apart from collusion
B. not the result of chance
C. not a guarantee of the accuracy of the facts
D. the result of a mass reaction of the witnesses

Questions 11-12.

DIRECTIONS: Questions 11 and 12 are to be answered SOLELY on the basis of the information given in the following paragraph.

The accuracy of the information about past occurrence obtainable in an interview is so low that one must take the stand that the best use to be made of the interview in this connection is a means of finding clues and avenues of access to more reliable sources of information. On the other hand, feelings and attitudes have been found to be clearly and correctly revealed in a properly conducted personal interview.

11. According to the above paragraph, information obtained in a personal interview   11.____

A. can be corroborated by other clues and more reliable sources of information revealed at the interview
B. can be used to develop leads to other sources of information about past events
C. is not reliable
D. is reliable if it relates to recent occurrences

12. According to the above paragraph, the personal interview is suitable for obtaining 12.____

    A. emotional reactions to a given situation
    B. fresh information on factors which may be forgotten
    C. revived recollection of previous events for later use as testimony
    D. specific information on material already reduced to writing

Questions 13-15.

DIRECTIONS: Questions 13 through 15 are to be answered on the basis of the following paragraph.

    Admissibility of handwriting standards (samples of handwriting for the purpose of comparison) as a basis for expert testimony is frequently necessary when the authenticity of disputed documents may be at issue. Under the older rules of common law, only that writing relating to the issues in the case could be used as a basis for handwriting testimony by an expert. Today, most jurisdictions admit irrelevant writings as standards for comparison. However, their genuineness, in all instances, must be established to the satisfaction of the court. There are a number of types of documents, however, not ordinarily relevant to the issues which are seldom acceptable to the court as handwriting standards, such as bail bonds, signatures on affidavits, depositions, etc. These are usually already before the court as part of the record in a case. Exhibits written in the presence of a witness or prepared voluntarily for a law enforcement officer are readily admissible in most jurisdictions. Testimony of a witness who is considered familiar with the writing is admissible in some jurisdictions. In criminal cases, it is possible that the signature on the fingerprint card obtained in connection with the arrest of the defendant for the crime currently charged may be admitted as a handwriting standard. In order to give the defendant the fairest possible treatment, most jurisdictions do not admit the signatures on fingerprint cards pertaining to prior arrests. However, they are admitted sometimes. In such instances, the court usually requires that the signature be photographed or removed from the card and no reference be made to the origin of the signature.

13. Of the following, the types of handwriting standards MOST likely to be admitted in evidence by most jurisdictions are those 13.____

    A. appearing on depositions and bail bonds
    B. which were written in the presence of a witness or voluntarily given to a law enforcement officer
    C. identified by witnesses who claim to be familiar with the handwriting
    D. which are in conformity with the rules of common law only

14. The PRINCIPAL factor which generally determines the acceptance of handwriting standards by the courts is 14.____

    A. the relevance of the submitted documents to the issues of the case
    B. the number of witnesses who have knowledge of the submitted documents
    C. testimony that the writing has been examined by a handwriting expert
    D. acknowledgment by the court of the authenticity of the submitted documents

15. The MOST logical reason for requiring the removal of the signature of a defendant from fingerprint cards pertaining to prior arrests, before admitting the signature in court as a handwriting standard, is that 15.____

A. it simplifies the process of identification of the signature as a standard for comparison
B. the need for identifying the fingerprints is eliminated
C. mention of prior arrests may be prejudicial to the defendant
D. a handwriting expert does not need information pertaining to prior arrests in order to make his identification

Questions 16-20.

DIRECTIONS: Questions 16 through 20 are to be answered SOLELY on the basis of the information contained in the following paragraph.

A statement which is offered in an attempt to prove the truth of the matters therein stated, but which is not made by the author as a witness before the court at the particular trial in which it is so offered, is hearsay. This is so whether the statement consists of words (oral or written), of symbols used as a substitute for words, or of signs or other conduct offered as the equivalent of a statement. Subject to some well-established exceptions, hearsay is not generally acceptable as evidence, and it does not become competent evidence just because it is received by the court without objection. One basis for this rule is simply that a fact cannot be proved by showing that somebody stated it was a fact. Another basis for the rule is the fundamental principle that in a criminal prosecution the testimony of the witness shall be taken before the court, so that at the time he gives the testimony offered in evidence he will be sworn and subject to cross-examination, the scrutiny of the court, and confrontation by the accused.

16. Which of the following is hearsay?   16.____
    A(n)

    A. written statement by a person not present at the court hearing where the statement is submitted as proof of an occurrence
    B. oral statement in court by a witness of what he saw
    C. written statement of what he saw by a witness present in court
    D. re-enactment by a witness in court of what he saw

17. In a criminal case, a statement by a person not present in court is   17.____

    A. *acceptable* evidence if not objected to by the prosecutor
    B. *acceptable* evidence if not objected to by the defense lawyer
    C. *not acceptable* evidence except in certain well-settled circumstances
    D. *not acceptable* evidence under any circumstances

18. The rule on hearsay is founded on the belief that   18.____

    A. proving someone said an act occurred is not proof that the act did occur
    B. a person who has knowledge about a case should be willing to appear in court
    C. persons not present in court are likely to be unreliable witnesses
    D. permitting persons to testify without appearing in court will lead to a disrespect for law

19. One reason for the general rule that a witness in a criminal case must give his testimony in court is that   19.____

    A.   a witness may be influenced by threats to make untrue statements
    B.   the opposite side is then permitted to question him
    C.   the court provides protection for a witness against unfair questioning
    D.   the adversary system is designed to prevent a miscarriage of justice

20. Of the following, the MOST appropriate title for the above passage would be   20.____

    A.   WHAT IS HEARSAY?   B.   RIGHTS OF DEFENDANTS
    C.   TRIAL PROCEDURES   D.   TESTIMONY OF WITNESSES

21. A person's statements are independent of who he is or what he is. Statements made by a person are not proved true or false by questioning his character or his position. A statement should stand or fall on its merits, regardless of who makes the statement. Truth is determined by evidence only. A person's character or personality should not be the determining factor in logic.   Discussions should not become incidents of name calling.
According to the above, whether or not a statement is true depends on the   21.____

    A.   recipient's conception of validity
    B.   maker's reliability
    C.   extent of support by facts
    D.   degree of merit the discussion has

Question 22-25.

DIRECTIONS: Questions 22 through 25 are to be answered on the basis of the following passage.

      The question, whether an act, repugnant to the Constitution, can become the law of the land, is a question deeply interesting to the United States; but, happily, not of an intricacy proportioned to its interest. It seems only necessary to recognize certain principles, supposed to have been long and well-established, to decide it. That the people have an original right to establish, for their future government, such principles as, in their opinion, shall most conduce to their own happiness, is the basis on which the whole American fabric has been erected. The exercise of this original right is a very great exertion; nor can it, nor ought it, to be frequently repeated. The principles, therefore, so established are deemed fundamental; and as the authority from which they proceed is supreme, and can seldom act, they are designed to be permanent.

22. The BEST title for the above passage would be   22.____

    A.   PRINCIPLES OF THE CONSTITUTION
    B.   THE ROOT OF CONSTITUTIONAL CHANGE
    C.   ONLY PEOPLE CAN CHANGE THE CONSTITUTION
    D.   METHODS OF CONSTITUTIONAL CHANGE

23. According to the above passage, original right is   23.____

    A.   fundamental to the principle that the people may choose their own form of government
    B.   established by the Constitution

C. the result of a very great exertion and should not often be repeated
D. supreme, can seldom act, and is designed to be permanent

24. Whether an act not in keeping with Constitutional principles can become law is, according to the above passage, 24.____

A. an intricate problem requiring great thought and concentration
B. determined by the proportionate interests of legislators
C. determined by certain long established principles, fundamental to Constitutional Law
D. an intricate problem, but less intricate than it would seem from the interest shown in it

25. According to the above passage, the phrase *and can seldom act* refers to the 25.____

A. principle early enacted into law by Americans when they chose their future form of government
B. original rights of the people as vested in the Constitution
C. original framers of the Constitution
D. established, fundamental principles of government

———

KEY (CORRECT ANSWERS)

1.	C		11.	B
2.	A		12.	A
3.	B		13.	B
4.	C		14.	D
5.	D		15.	C
6.	A		16.	A
7.	B		17.	C
8.	A		18.	A
9.	D		19.	B
10.	C		20.	A

21.	C
22.	B
23.	A
24.	D
25.	A

———

TEST 2

Questions 1-3.

DIRECTIONS: Questions 1 through 3 are to be answered SOLELY on the basis of the following paragraph.

The police laboratory performs a valuable service in crime investigation by assisting in the reconstruction of criminal action and by aiding in the identification of persons and things. When studied by a technician, physical things found at crime scenes often reveal facts useful in identifying the criminal and in determining what has occurred. The nature of substances to be examined and the character of the examination to be made vary so widely that the services of a large variety of skilled scientific persons are needed in crime investigations. To employ such a complete staff and to provide them with equipment and standards needed for all possible analysis and comparisons is beyond the means and the needs of any but the largest police departments. The search of crime scenes for physical evidence also calls for the services of specialists supplied with essential equipment and assigned to each tour of duty so as to provide service at any hour.

1. If a police department employs a large staff of technicians of various types in its laboratory, it will affect crime investigations to the extent that

    A. most crimes will be speedily solved
    B. identification of criminals will be aided
    C. search of crime scenes for physical evidence will become of less importance
    D. investigation by police officers will not usually be required

1.____

2. According to the above paragraph, the MOST complete study of objects found at the scenes of crimes is

    A. always done in all large police departments
    B. based on assigning one technician to each tour of duty
    C. probably done only in large police departments
    D. probably done in police departments of communities with low crime rates

2.____

3. According to the above paragraph, a large variety of skilled technicians is useful in criminal investigations because

    A. crimes cannot be solved without their assistance as part of the police team
    B. large police departments need large staffs
    C. many different kinds of tests on various substances can be made
    D. the police cannot predict what methods may be tried by wily criminals

3.____

Questions 4-6.

DIRECTIONS: Questions 4 through 6 are to be answered SOLELY on the basis of the following passage.

Probably the most important single mechanism for bringing the resources of science and technology to bear on the problems of crime would be the establishment of a major prestigious science and technology research program within a research institute. The program would create interdisciplinary teams of mathematicians, computer scientists, electronics engineers, physicists, biologists, and other natural scientists, psychologists, sociologists, economists, and lawyers. The institute and the program must be significant enough to attract the best scientists available, and, to this end, the director of this institute must himself have a background in science and technology and have the respect of scientists. Because it would be difficult to attract such a staff into the Federal government, the institute should be established by a university, a group of universities, or an independent nonprofit organization, and should be within a major metropolitan area. The institute would have to establish close ties with neighboring criminal justice agencies that would receive the benefit of serving as experimental laboratories for such an institute. In fact, the proposal for the institute might be jointly submitted with the criminal justice agencies. The research program would require in order to bring together the necessary *critical mass* of competent staff an annual budget which might reach 5 million dollars, funded with at least three years of lead time to assure continuity. Such a major scientific and technological research institute should be supported by the Federal government.

4. Of the following, the MOST appropriate title for the foregoing passage is   4._____

    A. RESEARCH - AN INTERDISCIPLINARY APPROACH TO FIGHTING CRIME
    B. A CURRICULUM FOR FIGHTING CRIME
    C. THE ROLE OF THE UNIVERSITY IN THE FIGHT AGAINST CRIME
    D. GOVERNMENTAL SUPPORT OF CRIMINAL RESEARCH PROGRAMS

5. According to the above passage, in order to attract the best scientists available, the   5._____
    research institute should

    A. provide psychologists and sociologists to counsel individual members of interdisciplinary teams
    B. encourage close ties with neighboring criminal justice agencies
    C. be led by a person who is respected in the scientific community
    D. be directly operated and funded by the Federal government

6. The term *critical mass,* as used in the above passage, refers MAINLY to   6._____

    A. a staff which would remain for three years of continuous service to the institute
    B. staff members necessary to carry out the research program of the institute successfully
    C. the staff necessary to establish relations with criminal justice agencies which will serve as experimental laboratories for the institute
    D. a staff which would be able to assist the institute in raising adequate funds

Questions 7-9.

DIRECTIONS: Questions 7 through 9 are to be answered SOLELY on the basis of the following paragraph.

The use of modern scientific methods in the examination of physical evidence often provides information to the investigator which he could not otherwise obtain. This applies particularly to small objects and materials present in minute quantities or trace evidence because the quantities here are such that they may be overlooked without methodical searching, and often special means of detection are needed. Whenever two objects come in contact with one another, there is a transfer of material, however slight. Usually, the softer object will transfer to the harder, but the transfer may be mutual. The quantity of material transferred differs with the type of material involved and the more violent the contact the greater the degree of transference. Through scientific methods of determining physical properties and chemical composition, we can add to the facts observable by the investigator's unaided senses, and thereby increase the chances of identification.

7. According to the above paragraph, the amount of material transferred whenever two objects come in contact with one another

    A. varies directly with the softness of the objects involved
    B. varies directly with the violence of the contact of the objects
    C. is greater when two soft, rather than hard, objects come into violent contact with each other
    D. is greater when coarse-grained, rather than smooth-grained, materials are involved

8. According to the above paragraph, the PRINCIPAL reason for employing scientific methods in obtaining trace evidence is that

    A. other methods do not involve a methodical search of the crime scene
    B. scientific methods of examination frequently reveal physical evidence which did not previously exist
    C. the amount of trace evidence may be so sparse that other methods are useless
    D. trace evidence cannot be properly identified unless special means of detection are employed

9. According to the above paragraph, the one of the following statements which BEST describes the manner in which scientific methods of analyzing physical evidence assists the investigator is that such methods

    A. add additional valuable information to the investigator's own knowledge of complex and rarely occurring materials found as evidence
    B. compensate for the lack of important evidential material through the use of physical and chemical analyses
    C. make possible an analysis of evidence which goes beyond the ordinary capacity of the investigator's senses
    D. identify precisely those physical characteristics of the individual which the untrained senses of the investigator are unable to discern

Questions 10-13.

DIRECTIONS: Questions 10 through 13 are to be answered SOLELY on the basis of the information contained in the following paragraph.

Under the provisions of the Bank Protection Act of 1968, enacted July 8, 1968, each Federal banking supervisory agency, as of January 7, 1969, had to issue rules establishing minimum standards with which financial institutions under their control must comply with respect to the installation, maintenance, and operation of security devices and procedures, reasonable in cost, to discourage robberies, burglaries, and larcenies, and to assist in the identification and apprehension of persons who commit such acts. The rules set the time limits within which the affected banks and savings and loan associations must comply with the standards, and the rules require the submission of periodic reports on the steps taken. A violator of a rule under this Act is subject to a civil penalty not to exceed $100 for each day of the violation. The enforcement of these regulations rests with the responsible banking supervisory agencies.

10. The Bank Protection Act of 1968 was designed to
10._____

    A. provide Federal police protection for banks covered by the Act
    B. have organizations covered by the Act take precautions against criminals
    C. set up a system for reporting all bank robberies to the FBI
    D. insure institutions covered by the Act from financial loss due to robberies, burglaries, and larcenies

11. Under the provisions of the Bank Protection Act of 1968, each Federal banking supervisory agency was required to set up rules for financial institutions covered by the Act governing the
11._____

    A. hiring of personnel
    B. punishment of burglars
    C. taking of protective measures
    D. penalties for violations

12. Financial institutions covered by the Bank Protection Act of 1968 were required to
12._____

    A. file reports at regular intervals on what they had done to prevent theft
    B. identify and apprehend persons who commit robberies, burglaries, and larcenies
    C. draw up a code of ethics for their employees
    D. have fingerprints of their employees filed with the FBI

13. Under the provisions of the Bank Protection Act of 1968, a bank which is subject to the rules established under the Act and which violates a rule is liable to a penalty of NOT _____ than $100 for each _____.
13._____

    A. more; violation
    C. less; violation
    B. less; day of violation
    D. more; day of violation

Questions 14-17.

DIRECTIONS: Questions 14 through 17 are to be answered SOLELY on the basis of the following passage.

Specific measures for prevention of pilferage will be based on careful analysis of the conditions at each agency. The most practical and effective method to control casual pilferage is the establishment of psychological deterrents.

One of the most common means of discouraging casual pilferage is to search individuals leaving the agency at unannounced times and places. These spot searches may occasionally detect attempts at theft, but greater value is realized by bringing to the attention of individuals the fact that they may be apprehended if they do attempt the illegal removal of property.

An aggressive security education program is an effective means of convincing employees that they have much more to lose than they do to gain by engaging in acts of theft. It is important for all employees to realize that pilferage is morally wrong no matter how insignificant the value of the item which is taken. In establishing any deterrent to casual pilferage, security officers must not lose sight of the fact that most employees are honest and disapprove of thievery. Mutual respect between security personnel and other employees of the agency must be maintained if the facility is to be protected from other more dangerous forms of human hazards. Any security measure which infringes on the human rights or dignity of others will jeopardize, rather than enhance, the overall protection of the agency.

14. The $100,000 yearly inventory of an agency revealed that $50 worth of goods had been stolen; the only individuals with access to the stolen materials were the employees. Of the following measures, which would the author of the above passage MOST likely recommend to a security officer?   14.____

    A. Conduct an intensive investigation of all employees to find the culprit.
    B. Make a record of the theft, but take no investigative or disciplinary action against any employee.
    C. Place a tight security check on all future movements of personnel.
    D. Remove the remainder of the material to an area with much greater security.

15. What does the passage imply is the percentage of employees whom a security officer should expect to be honest?   15.____

    A. No employee can be expected to be honest all of the time
    B. Just 50%
    C. Less than 50%
    D. More than 50%

16. According to the above passage, the security officer would use which of the following methods to minimize theft in buildings with many exits when his staff is very small?   16.____

    A. Conduct an inventory of all material and place a guard near that which is most likely to be pilfered
    B. Inform employees of the consequences of legal prosecution for pilfering
    C. Close off the unimportant exits and have all his men concentrate on a few exits
    D. Place a guard at each exit and conduct a casual search of individuals leaving the premises

17. Of the following, the title BEST suited for this passage is   17.____

    A. CONTROL MEASURES FOR CASUAL PILFERING
    B. DETECTING THE POTENTIAL PILFERER
    C. FINANCIAL LOSSES RESULTING FROM PILFERING
    D. THE USE OF MORAL PERSUASION IN PHYSICAL SECURITY

Questions 18-24.

DIRECTIONS: Questions 18 through 24 are to be answered SOLELY on the basis of the following passage.

Burglar alarms are designed to detect intrusion automatically. Robbery alarms enable a victim of a robbery or an attack to signal for help. Such devices can be located in elevators, hallways, homes and apartments, businesses and factories, and subways, as well as on the street in high-crime areas. Alarms could deter some potential criminals from attacking targets so protected. If alarms were prevalent and not visible, then they might serve to suppress crime generally. In addition, of course, the alarms can summon the police when they are needed.

All alarms must perform three functions: sensing or initiation of the signal, transmission of the signal and annunciation of the alarm. A burglar alarm needs a sensor to detect human presence or activity in an unoccupied enclosed area like a building or a room. A robbery victim would initiate the alarm by closing a foot or wall switch, or by triggering a portable transmitter which would send the alarm signal to a remote receiver. The signal can sound locally as a loud noise to frighten away a criminal, or it can be sent silently by wire to a central agency. A centralized annunciator requires either private lines from each alarmed point, or the transmission of some information on the location of the signal.

18. A conclusion which follows LOGICALLY from the above passage is that   18._____

    A. burglar alarms employ sensor devices; robbery alarms make use of initiation devices
    B. robbery alarms signal intrusion without the help of the victim; burglar alarms require the victim to trigger a switch
    C. robbery alarms sound locally; burglar alarms are transmitted to a central agency
    D. the mechanisms for a burglar alarm and a robbery alarm are alike

19. According to the above passage, alarms can be located   19._____

    A. in a wide variety of settings
    B. only in enclosed areas
    C. at low cost in high-crime areas
    D. only in places where potential criminals will be deterred

20. According to the above passage, which of the following is ESSENTIAL if a signal is to be received in a central office?   20._____

    A. A foot or wall switch
    B. A noise-producing mechanism
    C. A portable reception device
    D. Information regarding the location of the source

21. According to the above passage, an alarm system can function WITHOUT a   21._____

    A. centralized annunciating device
    B. device to stop the alarm
    C. sensing or initiating device
    D. transmission device

22. According to the above passage, the purpose of robbery alarms is to   22._____

    A. find out automatically whether a robbery has taken place
    B. lower the crime rate in high-crime areas
    C. make a loud noise to frighten away the criminal
    D. provide a victim with the means to signal for help

23. According to the above passage, alarms might aid in lessening crime if they were

    A. answered promptly by police
    B. completely automatic
    C. easily accessible to victims
    D. hidden and widespread

23._____

24. Of the following, the BEST title for the above passage is

    A. DETECTION OF CRIME BY ALARMS
    B. LOWERING THE CRIME RATE
    C. SUPPRESSION OF CRIME
    D. THE PREVENTION OF ROBBERY

24._____

25. Although the rural crime reporting area is much less developed than that for cities and towns, current data are collected in sufficient volume to justify the generalization that rural crime rates are lower than those or urban communities.
According to this statement,

    A. better reporting of crime occurs in rural areas than in cities
    B. there appears to be a lower proportion of crime in rural areas than in cities
    C. cities have more crime than towns
    D. crime depends on the amount of reporting

25._____

KEY (CORRECT ANSWERS)

1.	B		11.	C
2.	C		12.	A
3.	C		13.	D
4.	A		14.	B
5.	C		15.	D
6.	B		16.	B
7.	B		17.	A
8.	C		18.	A
9.	C		19.	A
10.	B		20.	D

21.	A
22.	D
23.	D
24.	A
25.	B

GLOSSARY OF LEGAL TERMS

TABLE OF CONTENTS

GLOSSARY OF LEGAL TERMS

A

ACTION - "Action" includes a civil action and a criminal action.

A FORTIORI - A terra meaning you can reason one thing from the existence of certain facts.

A POSTERIORI - From what goes after; from effect to cause.

A PRIORI - From what goes before; from cause to effect.

AB INITIO - From the beginning.

ABATE - To diminish or put an end to.

ABET - To encourage the commission of a crime.

ABEYANCE - Suspension, temporary suppression.

ABIDE - To accept the consequences of.

ABJURE - To renounce; give up.

ABRIDGE - To reduce; contract; diminish.

ABROGATE - To annul, repeal, or destroy.

ABSCOND - To hide or absent oneself to avoid legal action.

ABSTRACT - A summary.

ABUT - To border on, to touch.

ACCESS - Approach; in real property law it means the right of the owner of property to the use of the highway or road next to his land, without obstruction by intervening property owners.

ACCESSORY - In criminal law, it means the person who contributes or aids in the commission of a crime.

ACCOMMODATED PARTY - One to whom credit is extended on the strength of another person signing a commercial paper.

ACCOMMODATION PAPER - A commercial paper to which the accommodating party has put his name.

ACCOMPLICE - In criminal law, it means a person who together with the principal offender commits a crime.

ACCORD - An agreement to accept something different or less than that to which one is entitled, which extinguishes the entire obligation.

ACCOUNT - A statement of mutual demands in the nature of debt and credit between parties.

ACCRETION - The act of adding to a thing; in real property law, it means gradual accumulation of land by natural causes.

ACCRUE - To grow to; to be added to.

ACKNOWLEDGMENT - The act of going before an official authorized to take acknowledgments, and acknowledging an act as one's own.

ACQUIESCENCE - A silent appearance of consent.

ACQUIT - To legally determine the innocence of one charged with a crime.

AD INFINITUM - Indefinitely.

AD LITEM - For the suit.

AD VALOREM - According to value.

ADJECTIVE LAW - Rules of procedure.

ADJUDICATION - The judgment given in a case.

ADMIRALTY - Court having jurisdiction over maritime cases.

ADULT - Sixteen years old or over (in criminal law).

ADVANCE - In commercial law, it means to pay money or render other value before it is due.

ADVERSE - Opposed; contrary.

ADVOCATE - (v.) To speak in favor of;
                  (n.) One who assists, defends, or pleads for another.

AFFIANT - A person who makes and signs an affidavit.

AFFIDAVIT - A written and sworn to declaration of facts, voluntarily made.

AFFINITY- The relationship between persons through marriage with the kindred of each other; distinguished from consanguinity, which is the relationship by blood.

AFFIRM - To ratify; also when an appellate court affirms a judgment, decree, or order, it means that it is valid and right and must stand as rendered in the lower court.

AFOREMENTIONED; AFORESAID - Before or already said.

AGENT - One who represents and acts for another.

AID AND COMFORT - To help; encourage.

ALIAS - A name not one's true name.

ALIBI - A claim of not being present at a certain place at a certain time.

ALLEGE - To assert.

ALLOTMENT - A share or portion.

AMBIGUITY - Uncertainty; capable of being understood in more than one way.

AMENDMENT - Any language made or proposed as a change in some principal writing.

AMICUS CURIAE - A friend of the court; one who has an interest in a case, although not a party in the case, who volunteers advice upon matters of law to the judge. For example, a brief amicus curiae.

AMORTIZATION - To provide for a gradual extinction of (a future obligation) in advance of maturity, especially, by periodic contributions to a sinking fund which will be adequate to discharge a debt or make a replacement when it becomes necessary.

ANCILLARY - Aiding, auxiliary.

ANNOTATION - A note added by way of comment or explanation.

ANSWER - A written statement made by a defendant setting forth the grounds of his defense.

ANTE - Before.

ANTE MORTEM - Before death.

APPEAL - The removal of a case from a lower court to one of superior jurisdiction for the purpose of obtaining a review.

APPEARANCE - Coming into court as a party to a suit.

APPELLANT - The party who takes an appeal from one court or jurisdiction to another (appellate) court for review.

APPELLEE - The party against whom an appeal is taken.

APPROPRIATE - To make a thing one's own.

APPROPRIATION - Prescribing the destination of a thing; the act of the legislature designating a particular fund, to be applied to some object of government expenditure.

APPURTENANT - Belonging to; accessory or incident to.

ARBITER - One who decides a dispute; a referee.

ARBITRARY - Unreasoned; not governed by any fixed rules or standard.

ARGUENDO - By way of argument.

ARRAIGN - To call the prisoner before the court to answer to a charge.

ASSENT - A declaration of willingness to do something in compliance with a request.

ASSERT - Declare.

ASSESS - To fix the rate or amount.

ASSIGN - To transfer; to appoint; to select for a particular purpose.

ASSIGNEE - One who receives an assignment.

ASSIGNOR - One who makes an assignment.

AT BAR - Before the court.

AT ISSUE - When parties in an action come to a point where one asserts something and the other denies it.

ATTACH - Seize property by court order and sometimes arrest a person.

ATTEST - To witness a will, etc.; act of attestation.

AVERMENT - A positive statement of facts.

B

BAIL - To obtain the release of a person from legal custody by giving security and promising that he shall appear in court; to deliver (goods, etc.) in trust to a person for a special purpose.

BAILEE - One to whom personal property is delivered under a contract of bailment.

BAILMENT - Delivery of personal property to another to be held for a certain purpose and to be returned when the purpose is accomplished.

BAILOR - The party who delivers goods to another, under a contract of bailment.

BANC (OR BANK) - Bench; the place where a court sits permanently or regularly; also the assembly of all the judges of a court.

BANKRUPT - An insolvent person, technically, one declared to be bankrupt after a bankruptcy proceeding.

BAR - The legal profession.

BARRATRY - Exciting groundless judicial proceedings.

BARTER - A contract by which parties exchange goods for other goods.

BATTERY - Illegal interfering with another's person.

BEARER - In commercial law, it means the person in possession of a commercial paper which is payable to the bearer.

BENCH - The court itself or the judge.

BENEFICIARY - A person benefiting under a will, trust, or agreement.

BEST EVIDENCE RULE,THE - Except as otherwise provided by statute, no evidence other than the writing itself is admissible to prove the content of a writing. This section shall be known and may be cited as the best evidence rule.

BEQUEST - A gift of personal property under a will.

BILL - A formal written statement of complaint to a court of justice; also, a draft of an act of the legislature before it becomes a law; also, accounts for goods sold, services rendered, or work done.

BONA FIDE - In or with good faith; honestly.

BOND - An instrument by which the maker promises to pay a sum of money to another, usually providing that upon performances of a certain condition the obligation shall be void.

BOYCOTT - A plan to prevent the carrying on of a business by wrongful means.

BREACH - The breaking or violating of a law, or the failure to carry out a duty.

BRIEF - A written document, prepared by a lawyer to serve as the basis of an argument upon a case in court, usually an appellate court.

BURDEN OF PRODUCING EVIDENCE - The obligation of a party to introduce evidence sufficient to avoid a ruling against him on the issue.

BURDEN OF PROOF - The obligation of a party to establish by evidence a requisite degree of belief concerning a fact in the mind of the trier of fact or the court. The burden of proof may require a party to raise a reasonable doubt concerning the existence of nonexistence of a fact or that he establish the existence or nonexistence of a fact by a preponderance of the evidence, by clear and convincing proof, or by proof beyond a reasonable doubt.

Except as otherwise provided by law, the burden of proof requires proof by a preponderance of the evidence.

BUSINESS, A - Shall include every kind of business, profession, occupation, calling or operation of institutions, whether carried on for profit or not.

BY-LAWS - Regulations, ordinances, or rules enacted by a corporation, association, etc., for its own government.

C

CANON - A doctrine; also, a law or rule, of a church or association in particular.

CAPIAS - An order to arrest.

CAPTION - In a pleading, deposition or other paper connected with a case in court, it is the heading or introductory clause which shows the names of the parties, name of the court, number of the case on the docket or calendar, etc.

CARRIER - A person or corporation undertaking to transport persons or property.

CASE - A general term for an action, cause, suit, or controversy before a judicial body.

CAUSE - A suit, litigation or action before a court.

CAVEAT EMPTOR - Let the buyer beware. This term expresses the rule that the purchaser of an article must examine, judge, and test it for himself, being bound to discover any obvious defects or imperfections.

CERTIFICATE - A written representation that some legal formality has been complied with.

CERTIORARI - To be informed of; the name of a writ issued by a superior court directing the lower court to send up to the former the record and proceedings of a case.

CHANGE OF VENUE - To remove place of trial from one place to another.

CHARGE - An obligation or duty; a formal complaint; an instruction of the court to the jury upon a case.

CHARTER - (n.) The authority by virtue of which an organized body acts;
        (v.) in mercantile law, it means to hire or lease a vehicle or vessel for transportation.

CHATTEL - An article of personal property.

CHATTEL MORTGAGE - A mortgage on personal property.

CIRCUIT - A division of the country, for the administration of justice; a geographical area served by a court.

CITATION - The act of the court by which a person is summoned or cited; also, a reference to legal authority.

CIVIL (ACTIONS)- It indicates the private rights and remedies of individuals in contrast to the word "criminal" (actions) which relates to prosecution for violation of laws.

CLAIM (n.) - Any demand held or asserted as of right.

CODICIL - An addition to a will.

CODIFY - To arrange the laws of a country into a code.

COGNIZANCE - Notice or knowledge.

COLLATERAL - By the side; accompanying; an article or thing given to secure performance of a promise.

COMITY - Courtesy; the practice by which one court follows the decision of another court on the same question.

COMMIT - To perform, as an act; to perpetrate, as a crime; to send a person to prison.

COMMON LAW - As distinguished from law created by the enactment of the legislature (called statutory law), it relates to those principles and rules of action which derive their authority solely from usages and customs of immemorial antiquity, particularly with reference to the ancient unwritten law of England. The written pronouncements of the common law are found in court decisions.

COMMUTE - Change punishment to one less severe.

COMPLAINANT - One who applies to the court for legal redress.

COMPLAINT - The pleading of a plaintiff in a civil action; or a charge that a person has committed a specified offense.

COMPROMISE - An arrangement for settling a dispute by agreement.

CONCUR - To agree, consent.

CONCURRENT - Running together, at the same time.

CONDEMNATION - Taking private property for public use on payment therefor.

CONDITION - Mode or state of being; a qualification or restriction.

CONDUCT - Active and passive behavior; both verbal and nonverbal.

CONFESSION - Voluntary statement of guilt of crime.

CONFIDENTIAL COMMUNICATION BETWEEN CLIENT AND LAWYER - Information transmitted between a client and his lawyer in the course of that relationship and in confidence by a means which, so far as the client is aware, discloses the information to no third persons other than those who are present to further the interest of the client in the consultation or those to whom disclosure is reasonably necessary for the transmission of the information or the accomplishment of the purpose for which the lawyer is consulted, and includes a legal opinion formed and the advice given by the lawyer in the course of that relationship.

CONFRONTATION - Witness testifying in presence of defendant.

CONSANGUINITY - Blood relationship.

CONSIGN - To give in charge; commit; entrust; to send or transmit goods to a merchant, factor, or agent for sale.

CONSIGNEE - One to whom a consignment is made.

CONSIGNOR - One who sends or makes a consignment.

CONSPIRACY - In criminal law, it means an agreement between two or more persons to commit an unlawful act.

CONSPIRATORS - Persons involved in a conspiracy.

CONSTITUTION - The fundamental law of a nation or state.

CONSTRUCTION OF GENDERS - The masculine gender includes the feminine and neuter.

CONSTRUCTION OF SINGULAR AND PLURAL - The singular number includes the plural; and the plural, the singular.

CONSTRUCTION OF TENSES - The present tense includes the past and future tenses; and the future, the present.

CONSTRUCTIVE - An act or condition assumed from other parts or conditions.

CONSTRUE - To ascertain the meaning of language.

CONSUMMATE - To complete.

CONTIGUOUS - Adjoining; touching; bounded by.

CONTINGENT - Possible, but not assured; dependent upon some condition.

CONTINUANCE - The adjournment or postponement of an action pending in a court.

CONTRA - Against, opposed to; contrary.

CONTRACT - An agreement between two or more persons to do or not to do a particular thing.

CONTROVERT - To dispute, deny.

CONVERSION - Dealing with the personal property of another as if it were one's own, without right.

CONVEYANCE - An instrument transferring title to land.

CONVICTION - Generally, the result of a criminal trial which ends in a judgment or sentence that the defendant is guilty as charged.

COOPERATIVE - A cooperative is a voluntary organization of persons with a common interest, formed and operated along democratic lines for the purpose of supplying services at cost to its members and other patrons, who contribute both capital and business.

CORPUS DELICTI - The body of a crime; the crime itself.

CORROBORATE - To strengthen; to add weight by additional evidence.

COUNTERCLAIM - A claim presented by a defendant in opposition to or deduction from the claim of the plaintiff.

COUNTY - Political subdivision of a state.

COVENANT - Agreement.

CREDIBLE - Worthy of belief.

CREDITOR - A person to whom a debt is owing by another person, called the "debtor."

CRIMINAL ACTION - Includes criminal proceedings.

CRIMINAL INFORMATION - Same as complaint.

CRITERION (sing.)

CRITERIA (plural) - A means or tests for judging; a standard or standards.

CROSS-EXAMINATION - Examination of a witness by a party other than the direct examiner upon a matter that is within the scope of the direct examination of the witness.

CULPABLE - Blamable.

CY-PRES - As near as (possible). The rule of *cy-pres* is a rule for the construction of instruments in equity by which the intention of the party is carried out *as near as may be, when it* would be impossible or illegal to give it literal effect.

D

DAMAGES - A monetary compensation, which may be recovered in the courts by any person who has suffered loss, or injury, whether to his person, property or rights through the unlawful act or omission or negligence of another.

DECLARANT - A person who makes a statement.

DE FACTO - In fact; actually but without legal authority.

DE JURE - Of right; legitimate; lawful.

DE MINIMIS - Very small or trifling.

DE NOVO - Anew; afresh; a second time.

DEBT - A specified sum of money owing to one person from another, including not only the obligation of the debtor to pay, but the right of the creditor to receive and enforce payment.

DECEDENT - A dead person.

DECISION - A judgment or decree pronounced by a court in determination of a case.

DECREE - An order of the court, determining the rights of all parties to a suit.

DEED - A writing containing a contract sealed and delivered; particularly to convey real property.

DEFALCATION - Misappropriation of funds.

DEFAMATION - Injuring one's reputation by false statements.

DEFAULT - The failure to fulfill a duty, observe a promise, discharge an obligation, or perform an agreement.

DEFENDANT - The person defending or denying; the party against whom relief or recovery is sought in an action or suit.

DEFRAUD - To practice fraud; to cheat or trick.

DELEGATE (v.)- To entrust to the care or management of another.

DELICTUS - A crime.

DEMUR (v.) - To dispute the sufficiency in law of the pleading of the other side.

DEMURRAGE - In maritime law, it means, the sum fixed or allowed as remuneration to the owners of a ship for the detention of their vessel beyond the number of days allowed for loading and unloading or for sailing; also used in railroad terminology.

DENIAL - A form of pleading; refusing to admit the truth of a statement, charge, etc.

DEPONENT - One who gives testimony under oath reduced to writing.

DEPOSITION - Testimony given under oath outside of court for use in court or for the purpose of obtaining information in preparation for trial of a case.

DETERIORATION - A degeneration such as from decay, corrosion or disintegration.

DETRIMENT - Any loss or harm to person or property.

DEVIATION - A turning aside.

DEVISE - A gift of real property by the last will and testament of the donor.

DICTUM (sing.)

DICTA (plural) - Any statements made by the court in an opinion concerning some rule of law not necessarily involved nor essential to the determination of the case.

DIRECT EVIDENCE - Evidence that directly proves a fact, without an inference or presumption, and which in itself if true, conclusively establishes that fact.

DIRECT EXAMINATION - The first examination of a witness upon a matter that is not within the scope of a previous examination of the witness.

DISAFFIRM - To repudiate.

DISMISS - In an action or suit, it means to dispose of the case without any further consideration or hearing.

DISSENT - To denote disagreement of one or more judges of a court with the decision passed by the majority upon a case before them.

DOCKET (n.) - A formal record, entered in brief, of the proceedings in a court.

DOCTRINE - A rule, principle, theory of law.

DOMICILE - That place where a man has his true, fixed and permanent home to which whenever he is absent he has the intention of returning.

DRAFT (n.) - A commercial paper ordering payment of money drawn by one person on another.

DRAWEE - The person who is requested to pay the money.

DRAWER - The person who draws the commercial paper and addresses it to the drawee.

DUPLICATE - A counterpart produced by the same impression as the original enlargements and miniatures, or by mechanical or electronic re-recording, or by chemical reproduction, or by other equivalent technique which accurately reproduces the original.

DURESS - Use of force to compel performance or non-performance of an act.

E

EASEMENT - A liberty, privilege, or advantage without profit, in the lands of another.

EGRESS - Act or right of going out or leaving; emergence.

EIUSDEM GENERIS - Of the same kind, class or nature. A rule used in the construction of language in a legal document.

EMBEZZLEMENT - To steal; to appropriate fraudulently to one's own use property entrusted to one's care.

EMBRACERY - Unlawful attempt to influence jurors, etc., but not by offering value.

EMINENT DOMAIN - The right of a state to take private property for public use.

ENACT - To make into a law.

ENDORSEMENT - Act of writing one's name on the back of a note, bill or similar written instrument.

ENJOIN - To require a person, by writ of injunction from a court of equity, to perform or to abstain or desist from some act.

ENTIRETY - The whole; that which the law considers as one whole, and not capable of being divided into parts.

ENTRAPMENT - Inducing one to commit a crime so as to arrest him.

ENUMERATED - Mentioned specifically; designated.

ENURE - To operate or take effect.

EQUITY - In its broadest sense, this term denotes the spirit and the habit of fairness, justness, and right dealing which regulate the conduct of men.

ERROR - A mistake of law, or the false or irregular application of law as will nullify the judicial proceedings.

ESCROW - A deed, bond or other written engagement, delivered to a third person, to be delivered by him only upon the performance or fulfillment of some condition.

ESTATE - The interest which any one has in lands, or in any other subject of property.

ESTOP - To stop, bar, or impede.

ESTOPPEL - A rule of law which prevents a man from alleging or denying a fact, because of his own previous act.

ET AL. (alii) - And others.

ET SEQ. (sequential) - And the following.

ET UX. (uxor) - And wife.

EVIDENCE - Testimony, writings, material objects, or other things presented to the senses that are offered to prove the existence or non-existence of a fact.

Means from which inferences may be drawn as a basis of proof in duly constituted judicial or fact finding tribunals, and includes testimony in the form of opinion and hearsay.

EX CONTRACTU

EX DELICTO - In law, rights and causes of action are divided into two classes, those arising *ex contractu* (from a contract) and those arising *ex delicto* (from a delict or tort).

EX OFFICIO - From office; by virtue of the office.

EX PARTE - On one side only; by or for one.

EX POST FACTO - After the fact.

EX POST FACTO LAW - A law passed after an act was done which retroactively makes such act a crime.

EX REL. (relations) - Upon relation or information.

EXCEPTION - An objection upon a matter of law to a decision made, either before or after judgment by a court.

EXECUTOR (male)

EXECUTRIX (female) - A person who has been appointed by will to execute the will.

EXECUTORY - That which is yet to be executed or performed.

EXEMPT - To release from some liability to which others are subject.

EXONERATION - The removal of a burden, charge or duty.

EXTRADITION - Surrender of a fugitive from one nation to another.

F

F.A.S.- "Free alongside ship"; delivery at dock for ship named.

F.O.B.- "Free on board"; seller will deliver to car, truck, vessel, or other conveyance by which goods are to be transported, without expense or risk of loss to the buyer or consignee.

FABRICATE - To construct; to invent a false story.

FACSIMILE - An exact or accurate copy of an original instrument.

FACTOR - A commercial agent.

FEASANCE - The doing of an act.

FELONIOUS - Criminal, malicious.

FELONY - Generally, a criminal offense that may be punished by death or imprisonment for more than one year as differentiated from a misdemeanor.

FEME SOLE - A single woman.

FIDUCIARY - A person who is invested with rights and powers to be exercised for the benefit of another person.

FIERI FACIAS - A writ of execution commanding the sheriff to levy and collect the amount of a judgment from the goods and chattels of the judgment debtor.

FINDING OF FACT - Determination from proof or judicial notice of the existence of a fact. A ruling implies a supporting finding of fact; no separate or formal finding is required unless required by a statute of this state.

FISCAL - Relating to accounts or the management of revenue.

FORECLOSURE (sale) - A sale of mortgaged property to obtain satisfaction of the mortgage out of the sale proceeds.

FORFEITURE - A penalty, a fine.

FORGERY - Fabricating or producing falsely, counterfeited.

FORTUITOUS - Accidental.

FORUM - A court of justice; a place of jurisdiction.

FRAUD - Deception; trickery.

FREEHOLDER - One who owns real property.

FUNGIBLE - Of such kind or nature that one specimen or part may be used in the place of another.

G

GARNISHEE - Person garnished.

GARNISHMENT - A legal process to reach the money or effects of a defendant, in the posses-sion or control of a third person.

GRAND JURY - Not less than 16, not more than 23 citizens of a county sworn to inquire into crimes committed or triable in the county.

GRANT - To agree to; convey, especially real property.

GRANTEE - The person to whom a grant is made.

GRANTOR - The person by whom a grant is made.

GRATUITOUS - Given without a return, compensation or consideration.

GRAVAMEN - The grievance complained of or the substantial cause of a criminal action.

GUARANTY (n.) - A promise to answer for the payment of some debt, or the performance of some duty, in case of the failure of another person, who, in the first instance, is liable for such payment or performance.

GUARDIAN - The person, committee, or other representative authorized by law to protect the person or estate or both of an incompetent (or of a *sui juris* person having a guardian) and to act for him in matters affecting his person or property or both. An incompetent is a person under disability imposed by law.

GUILTY - Establishment of the fact that one has committed a breach of conduct; especially, a violation of law.

H

HABEAS CORPUS - You have the body; the name given to a variety of writs, having for their object to bring a party before a court or judge for decision as to whether such person is being lawfully held prisoner.

HABENDUM - In conveyancing; it is the clause in a deed conveying land which defines the extent of ownership to be held by the grantee.

HEARING - A proceeding whereby the arguments of the interested parties are heared.

HEARSAY - A type of testimony given by a witness who relates, not what he knows personally, but what others have told hi, or what he has heard said by others.

HEARSAY RULE, THE - (a) "Hearsay evidence" is evidence of a statement that was made other than by a witness while testifying at the hearing and that is offered to prove the truth of the matter stated; (b) Except as provided by law, hearsay evidence is inadmissible; (c) This section shall be known and may be cited as the hearsay rule.

HEIR - Generally, one who inherits property, real or personal.

HOLDER OF THE PRIVILEGE - (a) The client when he has no guardian or conservator; (b) A guardian or conservator of the client when the client has a guardian or conservator; (c) The personal representative of the client if the client is dead; (d) A successor, assign, trustee in dissolution, or any similar representative of a firm, association, organization, partnership, business trust, corporation, or public entity that is no longer in existence.

HUNG JURY - One so divided that they can't agree on a verdict.

HUSBAND-WIFE PRIVILEGE - An accused in a criminal proceeding has a privilege to prevent his spouse from testifying against him.

HYPOTHECATE - To pledge a thing without delivering it to the pledgee.

HYPOTHESIS - A supposition, assumption, or toehry.

I

I.E. (id est) - That is.

IB., OR IBID.(ibidem) - In the same place; used to refer to a legal reference previously cited to avoid repeating the entire citation.

ILLICIT - Prohibited; unlawful.

ILLUSORY - Deceiving by false appearance.

IMMUNITY - Exemption.

IMPEACH - To accuse, to dispute.

IMPEDIMENTS - Disabilities, or hindrances.

IMPLEAD - To sue or prosecute by due course of law.

IMPUTED - Attributed or charged to.

IN LOCO PARENTIS - In place of parent, a guardian.

IN TOTO - In the whole; completely.

INCHOATE - Imperfect; unfinished.

INCOMMUNICADO - Denial of the right of a prisoner to communicate with friends or relatives.

INCOMPETENT - One who is incapable of caring for his own affairs because he is mentally deficient or undeveloped.

INCRIMINATION - A matter will incriminate a person if it constitutes, or forms an essential part of, or, taken in connection with other matters disclosed, is a basis for a reasonable inference of such a violation of the laws of this State as to subject him to liability to punishment therefor, unless he has become for any reason permanently immune from punishment for such violation.

INCUMBRANCE - Generally a claim, lien, charge or liability attached to and binding real property.

INDEMNIFY - To secure against loss or damage; also, to make reimbursement to one for a loss already incurred by him.

INDEMNITY - An agreement to reimburse another person in case of an anticipated loss falling upon him.

INDICIA - Signs; indications.

INDICTMENT - An accusation in writing found and presented by a grand jury charging that a person has committed a crime.

INDORSE - To write a name on the back of a legal paper or document, generally, a negotiable instrument

INDUCEMENT - Cause or reason why a thing is done or that which incites the person to do the act or commit a crime; the motive for the criminal act.

INFANT - In civil cases one under 21 years of age.

INFORMATION - A formal accusation of crime made by a prosecuting attorney.

INFRA - Below, under; this word occurring by itself in a publication refers the reader to a future part of the publication.

INGRESS - The act of going into.

INJUNCTION - A writ or order by the court requiring a person, generally, to do or to refrain from doing an act.

INSOLVENT - The condition of a person who is unable to pay his debts.

INSTRUCTION - A direction given by the judge to the jury concerning the law of the case.

INTERIM - In the meantime; time intervening.

INTERLOCUTORY - Temporary, not final; something intervening between the commencement and the end of a suit which decides some point or matter, but is not a final decision of the whole controversy.

INTERROGATORIES - A series of formal written questions used in the examination of a party or a witness usually prior to a trial.

INTESTATE - A person who dies without a will.

INURE - To result, to take effect.

IPSO FACTO - By the fact iself; by the mere fact.

ISSUE (n.) The disputed point or question in a case,

J

JEOPARDY - Danger, hazard, peril.

JOINDER - Joining; uniting with another person in some legal steps or proceeding.

JOINT - United; combined.

JUDGE - Member or members or representative or representatives of a court conducting a trial or hearing at which evidence is introduced.

JUDGMENT - The official decision of a court of justice.

JUDICIAL OR JUDICIARY - Relating to or connected with the administration of justice.

JURAT - The clause written at the foot of an affidavit, stating when, where and before whom such affidavit was sworn.

JURISDICTION - The authority to hear and determine controversies between parties.

JURISPRUDENCE - The philosophy of law.

JURY - A body of persons legally selected to inquire into any matter of fact, and to render their verdict according to the evidence.

L

LACHES - The failure to diligently assert a right, which results in a refusal to allow relief.

LANDLORD AND TENANT - A phrase used to denote the legal relation existing between the owner and occupant of real estate.

LARCENY - Stealing personal property belonging to another.

LATENT - Hidden; that which does not appear on the face of a thing.

LAW - Includes constitutional, statutory, and decisional law.

LAWYER-CLIENT PRIVILEGE - (1) A "client" is a person, public officer, or corporation, association, or other organization or entity, either public or private, who is rendered professional legal services by a lawyer, or who consults a lawyer with a view to obtaining professional legal services from him; (2) A "lawyer" is a person authorized, or reasonably believed by the client to be authorized, to practice law in any state or nation; (3) A "representative of the lawyer" is one employed to assist the lawyer in the rendition of professional legal services; (4) A communication is "confidential" if not intended to be disclosed to third persons other than those to whom disclosure is in furtherance of the rendition of professional legal services to the client or those reasonably necessary for the transmission of the communication.

> *General rule of privilege* - A client has a privilege to refuse to disclose and to prevent any other person from disclosing confidential communications made for the purpose of facilitating the rendition of professional legal services to the client, (1) between himself or his representative and his lawyer or his lawyer's representative, or (2) between his lawyer and the lawyer's representative, or (3) by him or his lawyer to a lawyer representing another in a matter of common interest, or (4) between representatives of the client or between the client and a representative of the client, or (5) between lawyers representing the client.

LEADING QUESTION - Question that suggests to the witness the answer that the examining party desires.

LEASE - A contract by which one conveys real estate for a limited time usually for a specified rent; personal property also may be leased.

LEGISLATION - The act of enacting laws.

LEGITIMATE - Lawful.

LESSEE - One to whom a lease is given.

LESSOR - One who grants a lease

LEVY - A collecting or exacting by authority.

LIABLE - Responsible; bound or obligated in law or equity.

LIBEL (v.) - To defame or injure a person's reputation by a published writing.

> (n.) - The initial pleading on the part of the plaintiff in an admiralty proceeding.

LIEN - A hold or claim which one person has upon the property of another as a security for some debt or charge.

LIQUIDATED - Fixed; settled.

LIS PENDENS - A pending civil or criminal action.

LITERAL - According to the language.

LITIGANT - A party to a lawsuit.

LITATION - A judicial controversy.

LOCUS - A place.

LOCUS DELICTI - Place of the crime.

LOCUS POENITENTIAE - The abandoning or giving up of one's intention to commit some crime before it is fully completed or abandoning a conspiracy before its purpose is accomplished.

M

MALFEASANCE - To do a wrongful act.

MALICE - The doing of a wrongful act Intentionally without just cause or excuse.

MANDAMUS - The name of a writ issued by a court to enforce the performance of some public duty.

MANDATORY (adj.) Containing a command.

MARITIME - Pertaining to the sea or to commerce thereon.

MARSHALING - Arranging or disposing of in order.

MAXIM - An established principle or proposition.

MINISTERIAL - That which involves obedience to instruction, but demands no special discretion, judgment or skill.

MISAPPROPRIATE - Dealing fraudulently with property entrusted to one.

MISDEMEANOR - A crime less than a felony and punishable by a fine or imprisonment for less than one year.

MISFEASANCE - Improper performance of a lawful act.

MISREPRESENTATION - An untrue representation of facts.

MITIGATE - To make or become less severe, harsh.

MITTIMUS - A warrant of commitment to prison.

MOOT (adj.) Unsettled, undecided, not necessary to be decided.

MORTGAGE - A conveyance of property upon condition, as security for the payment of a debt or the performance of a duty, and to become void upon payment or performance according to the stipulated terms.

MORTGAGEE - A person to whom property is mortgaged.

MORTGAGOR - One who gives a mortgage.

MOTION - In legal proceedings, a "motion" is an application, either written or oral, addressed to the court by a party to an action or a suit requesting the ruling of the court on a matter of law.

MUTUALITY - Reciprocation.

N

NEGLIGENCE - The failure to exercise that degree of care which an ordinarily prudent person would exercise under like circumstances.

NEGOTIABLE (instrument) - Any instrument obligating the payment of money which is transferable from one person to another by endorsement and delivery or by delivery only.

NEGOTIATE - To transact business; to transfer a negotiable instrument; to seek agreement for the amicable disposition of a controversy or case.

NOLLE PROSEQUI - A formal entry upon the record, by the plaintiff in a civil suit or the prosecuting officer in a criminal action, by which he declares that he "will no further prosecute" the case.

NOLO CONTENDERE - The name of a plea in a criminal action, having the same effect as a plea of guilty; but not constituting a direct admission of guilt.

NOMINAL - Not real or substantial.

NOMINAL DAMAGES - Award of a trifling sum where no substantial injury is proved to have been sustained.

NONFEASANCE - Neglect of duty.

NOVATION - The substitution of a new debt or obligation for an existing one.

NUNC PRO TUNC - A phrase applied to acts allowed to be done after the time when they should be done, with a retroactive effect.("Now for then.")

O

OATH - Oath includes affirmation or declaration under penalty of perjury.

OBITER DICTUM - Opinion expressed by a court on a matter not essentially -involved in a case and hence not a decision; also called dicta, if plural.

OBJECT (v.) - To oppose as improper or illegal and referring the question of its propriety or legality to the court.

OBLIGATION - A legal duty, by which a person is bound to do or not to do a certain thing.

OBLIGEE - The person to whom an obligation is owed.

OBLIGOR - The person who is to perform the obligation.

OFFER (v.) - To present for acceptance or rejection.

      (n.) - A proposal to do a thing, usually a proposal to make a contract.

OFFICIAL INFORMATION - Information within the custody or control of a department or agency of the government the disclosure of which is shown to be contrary to the public interest.

OFFSET - A deduction.

ONUS PROBANDI - Burden of proof.

OPINION - The statement by a judge of the decision reached in a case, giving the law as applied to the case and giving reasons for the judgment; also a belief or view.

OPTION - The exercise of the power of choice; also a privilege existing in one person, for which he has paid money, which gives him the right to buy or sell real or personal property at a given price within a specified time.

ORDER - A rule or regulation; every direction of a court or judge made or entered in writing but not including a judgment.

ORDINANCE - Generally, a rule established by authority; also commonly used to designate the legislative acts of a municipal corporation.

ORIGINAL - Writing or recording itself or any counterpart intended to have the same effect by a person executing or issuing it. An "original" of a photograph includes the negative or any print therefrom. If data are stored in a computer or similar device, any printout or other output readable by sight, shown to reflect the data accurately, is an "original."

OVERT - Open, manifest.

P

PANEL - A group of jurors selected to serve during a term of the court.

PARENS PATRIAE - Sovereign power of a state to protect or be a guardian over children and incompetents.

PAROL - Oral or verbal.

PAROLE - To release one in prison before the expiration of his sentence, conditionally.

PARITY - Equality in purchasing power between the farmer and other segments of the economy.

PARTITION - A legal division of real or personal property between one or more owners.

PARTNERSHIP - An association of two or more persons to carry on as co-owners a business for profit.

PATENT (adj.) - Evident.

      (n.) - A grant of some privilege, property, or authority, made by the government or sovereign of a country to one or more individuals.

PECULATION - Stealing.

PECUNIARY - Monetary.

PENULTIMATE - Next to the last.

PER CURIAM - A phrase used in the report of a decision to distinguish an opinion of the whole court from an opinion written by any one judge.

PER SE - In itself; taken alone.

PERCEIVE - To acquire knowledge through one's senses.

PEREMPTORY - Imperative; absolute.

PERJURY - To lie or state falsely under oath.

PERPETUITY - Perpetual existence; also the quality or condition of an estate limited so that it will not take effect or vest within the period fixed by law.

PERSON - Includes a natural person, firm, association, organization, partnership, business trust, corporation, or public entity.

PERSONAL PROPERTY - Includes money, goods, chattels, things in action, and evidences of debt.

PERSONALTY - Short term for personal property.

PETITION - An application in writing for an order of the court, stating the circumstances upon which it is founded and requesting any order or other relief from a court.

PLAINTIFF - A person who brings a court action.

PLEA - A pleading in a suit or action.

PLEADINGS - Formal allegations made by the parties of their respective claims and defenses, for the judgment of the court.

PLEDGE - A deposit of personal property as a security for the performance of an act.

PLEDGEE - The party to whom goods are delivered in pledge.

PLEDGOR - The party delivering goods in pledge.

PLENARY - Full; complete.

POLICE POWER - Inherent power of the state or its political subdivisions to enact laws within constitutional limits to promote the general welfare of society or the community.

POLLING THE JURY - Call the names of persons on a jury and requiring each juror to declare what his verdict is before it is legally recorded.

POST MORTEM - After death.

POWER OF ATTORNEY - A writing authorizing one to act for another.

PRECEPT - An order, warrant, or writ issued to an officer or body of officers, commanding him or them to do some act within the scope of his or their powers.

PRELIMINARY FACT - Fact upon the existence or nonexistence of which depends the admissibility or inadmissibility of evidence. The phrase "the admissibility or inadmissibility of evidence" includes the qualification or disqualification of a person to be a witness and the existence or non-existence of a privilege.

PREPONDERANCE - Outweighing.

PRESENTMENT - A report by a grand jury on something they have investigated on their own knowledge.

PRESUMPTION - An assumption of fact resulting from a rule of law which requires such fact to be assumed from another fact or group of facts found or otherwise established in the action.

PRIMA FACUE - At first sight.

PRIMA FACIE CASE - A case where the evidence is very patent against the defendant.

PRINCIPAL - The source of authority or rights; a person primarily liable as differentiated from "principle" as a primary or basic doctrine.

PRO AND CON - For and against.

PRO RATA - Proportionally.

PROBATE - Relating to proof, especially to the proof of wills.

PROBATIVE - Tending to prove.

PROCEDURE - In law, this term generally denotes rules which are established by the Federal, State, or local Governments regarding the types of pleading and courtroom practice which must be followed by the parties involved in a criminal or civil case.

PROCLAMATION - A public notice by an official of some order, intended action, or state of facts.

PROFFERED EVIDENCE - The admissibility or inadmissibility of which is dependent upon the existence or nonexistence of a preliminary fact.

PROMISSORY (NOTE) - A promise in writing to pay a specified sum at an expressed time, or on demand, or at sight, to a named person, or to his order, or bearer.

PROOF - The establishment by evidence of a requisite degree of belief concerning a fact in the mind of the trier of fact or the court.

PROPERTY - Includes both real and personal property.

PROPRIETARY (adj.) - Relating or pertaining to ownership; usually a single owner.

PROSECUTE - To carry on an action or other judicial proceeding; to proceed against a person criminally.

PROVISO - A limitation or condition in a legal instrument.

PROXIMATE - Immediate; nearest

PUBLIC EMPLOYEE - An officer, agent, or employee of a public entity.

PUBLIC ENTITY - Includes a national, state, county, city and county, city, district, public authority, public agency, or any other political subdivision or public corporation, whether foreign or domestic.

PUBLIC OFFICIAL - Includes an official of a political dubdivision of such state or territory and of a municipality.

PUNITIVE - Relating to punishment.

Q

QUASH - To make void.

QUASI - As if; as it were.

QUID PRO QUO - Something for something; the giving of one valuable thing for another.

QUITCLAIM (v.) - To release or relinquish claim or title to, especially in deeds to realty.

QUO WARRANTO - A legal procedure to test an official's right to a public office or the right to hold a franchise, or to hold an office in a domestic corporation.

R

RATIFY - To approve and sanction.

REAL PROPERTY - Includes lands, tenements, and hereditaments.

REALTY - A brief term for real property.

REBUT - To contradict; to refute, especially by evidence and arguments.

RECEIVER - A person who is appointed by the court to receive, and hold in trust property in litigation.

RECIDIVIST - Habitual criminal.

RECIPROCAL - Mutual.

RECOUPMENT - To keep back or get something which is due; also, it is the right of a defendant to have a deduction from the amount of the plaintiff's damages because the plaintiff has not fulfilled his part of the same contract.

RECROSS EXAMINATION - Examination of a witness by a cross-examiner subsequent to a redirect examination of the witness.

REDEEM - To release an estate or article from mortgage or pledge by paying the debt for which it stood as security.

REDIRECT EXAMINATION - Examination of a witness by the direct examiner subsequent to the cross-examination of the witness.

REFEREE - A person to whom a cause pending in a court is referred by the court, to take testimony, hear the parties, and report thereon to the court.

REFERENDUM - A method of submitting an important legislative or administrative matter to a direct vote of the people.

RELEVANT EVIDENCE - Evidence including evidence relevant to the credulity of a witness or hearsay declarant, having any tendency in reason to prove or disprove any disputed fact that is of consequence to the determination of the action.

REMAND - To send a case back to the lower court from which it came, for further proceedings.

REPLEVIN - An action to recover goods or chattels wrongfully taken or detained.

REPLY (REPLICATION) - Generally, a reply is what the plaintiff or other person who has instituted proceedings says in answer to the defendant's case.

RE JUDICATA - A thing judicially acted upon or decided.

RES ADJUDICATA - Doctrine that an issue or dispute litigated and determined in a case between the opposing parties is deemed permanently decided between these parties.

RESCIND (RECISSION) - To avoid or cancel a contract.

RESPONDENT - A defendant in a proceeding in chancery or admiralty; also, the person who contends against the appeal in a case.

RESTITUTION - In equity, it is the restoration of both parties to their original condition (when practicable), upon the rescission of a contract for fraud or similar cause.

RETROACTIVE (RETROSPECTIVE) - Looking back; effective as of a prior time.

REVERSED - A term used by appellate courts to indicate that the decision of the lower court in the case before it has been set aside.

REVOKE - To recall or cancel.

RIPARIAN (RIGHTS) - The rights of a person owning land containing or bordering on a water course or other body of water, such as lakes and rivers.

S

SALE - A contract whereby the ownership of property is transferred from one person to another for a sum of money or for any consideration.

SANCTION - A penalty or punishment provided as a means of enforcing obedience to a law; also, an authorization.

SATISFACTION - The discharge of an obligation by paying a party what is due to him; or what is awarded to him by the judgment of a court or otherwise.

SCIENTER - Knowingly; also, it is used in pleading to denote the defendant 's guilty knowledge.

SCINTILLA - A spark; also the least particle.

SECRET OF STATE - Governmental secret relating to the national defense or the international relations of the United States.

SECURITY - Indemnification; the term is applied to an obligation, such as a mortgage or deed of trust, given by a debtor to insure the payment or performance of his debt, by furnishing the creditor with a resource to be used in case of the debtor's failure to fulfill the principal obligation.

SENTENCE - The judgment formally pronounced by the court or judge upon the defendant after his conviction in a criminal prosecution.

SET-OFF - A claim or demand which one party in an action credits against the claim of the opposing party.

SHALL and MAY - "Shall" is mandatory and "may" is permissive.

SITUS - Location.

SOVEREIGN - A person, body or state in which independent and supreme authority is vested.

STARE DECISIS - To follow decided cases.

STATE - "State" means this State, unless applied to the different parts of the United States. In the latter case, it includes any state, district, commonwealth, territory or insular possession of the United States, including the District of Columbia.

STATEMENT - (a) Oral or written verbal expression or (b) nonverbal conduct of a person intended by him as a substitute for oral or written verbal expression.

STATUTE - An act of the legislature. Includes a treaty.

STATUTE OF LIMITATION - A statute limiting the time to bring an action after the right of action has arisen.

STAY - To hold in abeyance an order of a court.

STIPULATION - Any agreement made by opposing attorneys regulating any matter incidental to the proceedings or trial.

SUBORDINATION (AGREEMENT) - An agreement making one's rights inferior to or of a lower rank than another's.

SUBORNATION - The crime of procuring a person to lie or to make false statements to a court.

SUBPOENA - A writ or order directed to a person, and requiring his attendance at a particular time and place to testify as a witness.

SUBPOENA DUCES TECUM - A subpoena used, not only for the purpose of compelling witnesses to attend in court, but also requiring them to bring with them books or documents which may be in their possession, and which may tend to elucidate the subject matter of the trial.

SUBROGATION - The substituting of one for another as a creditor, the new creditor succeeding to the former's rights.

SUBSIDY - A government grant to assist a private enterprise deemed advantageous to the public.

SUI GENERIS - Of the same kind.

SUIT - Any civil proceeding by a person or persons against another or others in a court of justice by which the plaintiff pursues the remedies afforded him by law.

SUMMONS - A notice to a defendant that an action against him has been commenced and requiring him to appear in court and answer the complaint.

SUPRA - Above; this word occurring by itself in a book refers the reader to a previous part of the book.

SURETY - A person who binds himself for the payment of a sum of money, or for the performance of something else, for another.

SURPLUSAGE - Extraneous or unnecessary matter.

SURVIVORSHIP - A term used when a person becomes entitled to property by reason of his having survived another person who had an interest in the property.

SUSPEND SENTENCE - Hold back a sentence pending good behavior of prisoner.

SYLLABUS - A note prefixed to a report, especially a case, giving a brief statement of the court's ruling on different issues of the case.

T

TALESMAN - Person summoned to fill a panel of jurors.

TENANT - One who holds or possesses lands by any kind of right or title; also, one who has the temporary use and occupation of real property owned by another person (landlord), the duration and terms of his tenancy being usually fixed by an instrument called "a lease."

TENDER - An offer of money; an expression of willingness to perform a contract according to its terms.

TERM - When used with reference to a court, it signifies the period of time during which the court holds a session, usually of several weeks or months duration.

TESTAMENTARY - Pertaining to a will or the administration of a will.

TESTATOR (male)

TESTATRIX (female) - One who makes or has made a testament or will.

TESTIFY (TESTIMONY) - To give evidence under oath as a witness.

TO WIT - That is to say; namely.

TORT - Wrong; injury to the person.

TRANSITORY - Passing from place to place.

TRESPASS - Entry into another's ground, illegally.

TRIAL - The examination of a cause, civil or criminal, before a judge who has jurisdiction over it, according to the laws of the land.

TRIER OF FACT - Includes (a) the jury and (b) the court when the court is trying an issue of fact other than one relating to the admissibility of evidence.

TRUST - A right of property, real or personal, held by one party for the benefit of another.

TRUSTEE - One who lawfully holds property in custody for the benefit of another.

U

UNAVAILABLE AS A WITNESS - The declarant is (1) Exempted or precluded on the ground of privilege from testifying concerning the matter to which his statement is relevant; (2) Disqualified from testifying to the matter; (3) Dead or unable to attend or to testify at the hearing because of then existing physical or mental illness or infirmity; (4) Absent from the hearing and the court is unable to compel his attendance by its process; or (5) Absent from the hearing and the proponent of his statement has exercised reasonable diligence but has been unable to procure his attendance by the court's process.

ULTRA VIRES - Acts beyond the scope and power of a corporation, association, etc.

UNILATERAL - One-sided; obligation upon, or act of one party.

USURY - Unlawful interest on a loan.

V

VACATE - To set aside; to move out.

VARIANCE - A discrepancy or disagreement between two instruments or two aspects of the same case, which by law should be consistent.

VENDEE - A purchaser or buyer.

VENDOR - The person who transfers property by sale, particularly real estate; the term "seller" is used more commonly for one who sells personal property.

VENIREMEN - Persons ordered to appear to serve on a jury or composing a panel of jurors.

VENUE - The place at which an action is tried, generally based on locality or judicial district in which an injury occurred or a material fact happened.

VERDICT - The formal decision or finding of a jury.

VERIFY - To confirm or substantiate by oath.

VEST - To accrue to.

VOID - Having no legal force or binding effect.

VOIR DIRE - Preliminary examination of a witness or a juror to test competence, interest, prejudice, etc.

W

WAIVE - To give up a right.

WAIVER - The intentional or voluntary relinquishment of a known right.

WARRANT (WARRANTY) (v.) - To promise that a certain fact or state of facts, in relation to the subject matter, is, or shall be, as it is represented to be.

WARRANT (n.) - A writ issued by a judge, or other competent authority, addressed to a sheriff, or other officer, requiring him to arrest the person therein named, and bring him before the judge or court to answer or be examined regarding the offense with which he is charged.

WRIT - An order or process issued in the name of the sovereign or in the name of a court or judicial officer, commanding the performance or nonperformance of some act.

WRITING - Handwriting, typewriting, printing, photostating, photographing and every other means of recording upon any tangible thing any form of communication or representation, including letters, words, pictures, sounds, or symbols, or combinations thereof.

WRITINGS AND RECORDINGS - Consists of letters, words, or numbers, or their equivalent, set down by handwriting, typewriting, printing, photostating, photographing, magnetic impulse, mechanical or electronic recording, or other form of data compilation.

Y

YEA AND NAY - Yes and no.

YELLOW DOG CONTRACT - A contract by which employer requires employee to sign an instrument promising as condition that he will not join a union during its continuance, and will be discharged if he does join.

Z

ZONING - The division of a city by legislative regulation into districts and the prescription and application in each district of regulations having to do with structural and architectural designs of buildings and of regulations prescribing use to which buildings within designated districts may be put.

ANSWER SHEET

TEST NO. _____ PART ___ TITLE OF POSITION _____

PLACE OF EXAMINATION _____

(CITY OR TOWN)   (STATE)   DATE _____

RATING

USE THE SPECIAL PENCIL. MAKE GLOSSY BLACK MARKS.

Make only ONE mark for each answer. Additional and stray marks may be counted as mistakes. In making corrections, erase errors COMPLETELY.

ANSWER SHEET

TEST NO. ______________ PART ______ TITLE OF POSITION ______________________________
(AS GIVEN IN EXAMINATION ANNOUNCEMENT - INCLUDE OPTION, IF ANY)

PLACE OF EXAMINATION ______________________________ (CITY OR TOWN) ______________ (STATE) DATE ______________

RATING

USE THE SPECIAL PENCIL. MAKE GLOSSY BLACK MARKS.

1 A B C D E	26 A B C D E	51 A B C D E	76 A B C D E	101 A B C D E
2 A B C D E	27 A B C D E	52 A B C D E	77 A B C D E	102 A B C D E
3 A B C D E	28 A B C D E	53 A B C D E	78 A B C D E	103 A B C D E
4 A B C D E	29 A B C D E	54 A B C D E	79 A B C D E	104 A B C D E
5 A B C D E	30 A B C D E	55 A B C D E	80 A B C D E	105 A B C D E
6 A B C D E	31 A B C D E	56 A B C D E	81 A B C D E	106 A B C D E
7 A B C D E	32 A B C D E	57 A B C D E	82 A B C D E	107 A B C D E
8 A B C D E	33 A B C D E	58 A B C D E	83 A B C D E	108 A B C D E
9 A B C D E	34 A B C D E	59 A B C D E	84 A B C D E	109 A B C D E
10 A B C D E	35 A B C D E	60 A B C D E	85 A B C D E	110 A B C D E

Make only ONE mark for each answer. Additional and stray marks may be counted as mistakes. In making corrections, erase errors COMPLETELY.

11 A B C D E	36 A B C D E	61 A B C D E	86 A B C D E	111 A B C D E
12 A B C D E	37 A B C D E	62 A B C D E	87 A B C D E	112 A B C D E
13 A B C D E	38 A B C D E	63 A B C D E	88 A B C D E	113 A B C D E
14 A B C D E	39 A B C D E	64 A B C D E	89 A B C D E	114 A B C D E
15 A B C D E	40 A B C D E	65 A B C D E	90 A B C D E	115 A B C D E
16 A B C D E	41 A B C D E	66 A B C D E	91 A B C D E	116 A B C D E
17 A B C D E	42 A B C D E	67 A B C D E	92 A B C D E	117 A B C D E
18 A B C D E	43 A B C D E	68 A B C D E	93 A B C D E	118 A B C D E
19 A B C D E	44 A B C D E	69 A B C D E	94 A B C D E	119 A B C D E
20 A B C D E	45 A B C D E	70 A B C D E	95 A B C D E	120 A B C D E
21 A B C D E	46 A B C D E	71 A B C D E	96 A B C D E	121 A B C D E
22 A B C D E	47 A B C D E	72 A B C D E	97 A B C D E	122 A B C D E
23 A B C D E	48 A B C D E	73 A B C D E	98 A B C D E	123 A B C D E
24 A B C D E	49 A B C D E	74 A B C D E	99 A B C D E	124 A B C D E
25 A B C D E	50 A B C D E	75 A B C D E	100 A B C D E	125 A B C D E